THE PRESIDENT'S FLAG

THE WHITE HOUSE

ATLAS of the

by

DONALD E. COOKE

PRESIDENTS

illustrated maps by
Dwight Dobbins

pictures of the presidents
based on photographs of portraits
supplied by The Library of Congress

INCORPORATED
MAPLEWOOD, NEW JERSEY

Contents

How to Prepare for the Presidency

by
John Fitzgerald Kennedy

Fred Blumenthal, Parade Publications correspondent, once asked President Kennedy this question: "Somewhere in our land today there is a high school or college student who will one day be sitting in your chair. If you could now speak to this future President, what advice and guidance would you give him or her?"

Following is the President's answer. This is the first time that an incumbent Chief Executive has given such frank counsel to a young American destined to succeed him. It is reproduced here by permission of Parade Publications, 733 Third Avenue, New York, New York.

The first lesson of the Presidency is that it is impossible to foretell the precise nature of the problems that will confront you or the specific skills and capacities which those problems will demand. It is an office which called upon a man of peace, Lincoln, to become a great leader in a bloody war; which required a profound believer in limiting the scope of federal government, Jefferson, to expand dramatically the powers and range of that government; which challenged a man dedicated to domestic social reform, Franklin Roosevelt, to lead this nation into a deep and irrevocable involvement in world affairs. And when you assume the Presidency you too will face problems, difficulties, crises and challenges which no one can now foresee.

In 1645, John Winthrop, Deputy Governor of Massachusetts Bay Colony, after a long and stormy trial acquitting him of impeachment for exceeding his authority, reminded his fellow citizens that "when you call one to be a magistrate, he doth not profess nor undertake to have sufficient skill for that office, nor can you furnish him with gifts . . . therefore you must run the hazard of his skill and ability."

This insight into the nature of governing affirms the lesson of our history that there is no program of vocational training for the Presidency; no specific area of knowledge that is peculiarly relevant. Nor are qualities of great leadership drawn from any particular section of the country or section of society. Nine of our Presidents, among them some of the most brilliant in office, did not attend college; whereas Thomas Jefferson was one of the great scholars of the age and Woodrow Wilson the president of Princeton University. We have had Presidents who were lawyers and soldiers and teachers. One was an engineer and another a journalist. They have been drawn from the wealthiest and most distinguished families of the nation, and have come from poor and anonymous beginnings. Some, seemingly well endowed with great abilities and fine qualities, were unable to cope with the demands of the office, while others rose to a greatness far beyond any expectation.

Thus I cannot counsel you about what subjects to study or what vocation to follow. But whatever you do you would be well advised to practice stern discipline and vigorous, unremitting effort. For high qualities and great achievements are not merely matters of chance or birth. They are the product of long and disciplined toil.

Yet, in a more general way, there are experiences which you can pursue, experiences which will support you in the conduct of your great office.

It will help you to know the country you seek to lead. It was one of the great strengths of a President such as Theodore Roosevelt that he knew and loved the diverse magnificence of our fields and mountain ranges, deserts and great rivers, our abundant farmlands and the thousand voices of our cities. No revolution in communication or transportation can destroy the fact that this continent is, as Whitman said, "a nation of nations," which you must see and know before you can govern.

Nor is it accidental that many of our outstanding Presidents, men such as Jefferson or Wilson or Truman, have had a deep sense of history. For of all the disciplines, the study of the folly and achievements of man is best calculated to help develop the critical sense of what is permanent and meaningful amid the mass of superficial and transient events and decisions which engulf the Presidency. And it is on this sense, more than any other, that great leadership depends.

Most important of all, and most difficult to consciously pursue, is an understanding of the people you will lead. You, and at times you alone, will be the spokesman for the great and often silent majority. And the final measure of your Administration will, in large measure, rest on how well you respond to their inward hopes while leading them toward new horizons of ambition and achievement. Perhaps you will derive this quality from your origins, as did Lincoln; or from the application of understanding and compassion to the problems of government, as did Franklin Roosevelt. Yet, although the possible sources of this understanding are many, if you find the opportunity to know and work with Americans of diverse backgrounds, occupations and beliefs, then I would urge you to take eagerly that opportunity to enrich yourself.

As a great world leader you will have problems and responsibilities which were not faced by Presidents throughout much of our history. As President of the United States you are a focus of the attention, ambitions and desires of people and nations throughout the world. It will help you to travel and to learn about these other lands. For the welfare and security of the United States, the future of your own country, is bound to your capacity to exercise leadership and judgment on a global scale.

The most important human qualities of leadership are best embodied in that most towering of American Presidents, Lincoln: a combination of humility and self-confidence, inner resolution and energy, which gives a President the capacity to listen to others, to be aware of his own limitations, but also to follow the command of John Adams that "In all great and essential measures the President is bound by honor and his conscience . . . to act his own mature and unbiased judgment." I can advise you to be aware of the importance of these qualities, but no one can tell you how to develop them. I only hope, for the welfare of our country, that you will possess them when you come to office.

No one can guarantee that if you follow this or any other advice you will become a great President. For the Presidency is peculiarly an office which is shaped by the individual who holds it. And greatness depends on the times as well as the man. But if you work toward your goal, practice discipline and unremitting effort, wish Godspeed to those who will hold and protect the great office of the Republic so that it may pass unimpaired to you and those who will follow you, then, if some chance keeps you from the Presidency, you will still know that you are prepared to serve well your nation as a citizen.

ATLAS
of the
PRESIDENTS

George Washington

In those early days of a new nation, before the advent of motion pictures, television and various marvels of recording and communication, the images of great men had to be drawn in broad strokes, and they were formed by the sheer power of personality, words, and actions. It is not surprising that Washington became known as the "father of his country," in view of the circumstances. But it is evident that he was precisely the man to assume the role that history assigned to him.

George Washington was a stern administrator, deeply religious, a stickler for rules, and a strict military disciplinarian. Yet he was not a haughty aristocrat. Here are some facts which shed a more human light upon him.

For one thing, he took command of a ragged army of revolutionaries. This was an act of courage and moral conviction that flew directly in the face of tradition and of what might have appeared to be good common sense.

Later, when Washington became president, he was able to hold together an explosive political situation. His calm wisdom and understanding helped him hammer out a model of sound administration for future chief executives to follow.

George Washington was born February 22, 1732, on a farm near Fredericksburg, Virginia. He had only six years of schooling, and his ambition was to become a sailor. He took his first job as a surveyor's helper at sixteen years of age. He was appointed official county surveyor a year later. At nineteen Washington was a major in the Virginia militia, and at twenty-three years of age he led all of Virginia's army.

His early experiences as a soldier included an ill-fated expedition as aide to General Braddock when the British soldiers marched against the French and Indians in 1755. Braddock ignored Washington's

warnings and led his force into an ambush near Fort Duquesne. Braddock was fatally wounded during the resulting rout of the British, but Washington escaped unhurt in spite of having "two horses shot under me."

Politics attracted him early in his career. He was a member of the Virginia House of Burgesses and of the Continental Congress before he took command of the American Revolutionary army.

It is doubtful that the colonists could have endured the long, frustrating war without the firm, unshakable leadership of a man like George Washington. Whatever his personal feelings must have been, in defeat after defeat, Washington maintained his dignity. The encampment at Valley Forge, Pa., during the bitter winter of 1777-1778, was a low point in the American army's fortunes, yet Washington's courage withstood the ordeal. How he managed to keep his ragged, dwindling forces together remains one of the mysteries and one of the miracles of history. In spite of every conceivable setback, Washington pulled the colonies through to victory in the Revolutionary War.

After the British surrender at Yorktown, October 19, 1781, George Washington returned to Mount Vernon. Later he was called upon to lead the Philadelphia convention which adopted the Constitution in 1787 He was made the first president of the United States by a unanimous vote of the electors and was inaugurated in New York City, April 30, 1789.

In his address, Washington said, ". . . the preservation of the sacred fire of liberty and the destiny of the republican model of government are justly considered, perhaps, as deeply, as finally, staked on the experiment entrusted to the hands of the American people."

Washington was reelected for a second term. He continued to build a strong government, solidly based on Constitutional law. In his farewell address in 1796, he wrote to his countrymen, "The basis of our political systems is the right of the people to make and to alter their constitutions of government. But the constitution which at any time exists till changed by an explicit and authentic act of the whole people is sacredly obligatory upon all."

Washington's dream of retirement at his beloved Mount Vernon lasted only three years. He died at 67, December 14, 1799, having contracted a severe cold while riding about his estate.

During Washington's administration the Departments of State, Treasury and War were formed. The Supreme Court was established and the first ten amendments to the Constitution, known as the Bill of Rights, were ratified by the states. Across the sea, France was in the throes of her own revolution and was at war with Austria and Prussia. The first U.S. Census showed a population of 3,929,214 when Vermont and Kentucky were admitted as states to the Union.

MOUNT VERNON

Voyage to West Indies 1751

BARBADOS

CANADA
(British)

VERMONT
14th State
1791

N.Y.

N.H.

MASS.

R.I.

CONN.

NEW YORK
Inauguration 1789

N.J.

Whisky
Rebellion 1794

PA.

MD.

DEL

VALLEY FORGE

TERRITORY NORTHWEST
OF THE OHIO RIVER

FORT DUQUESNE

MOUNT VERNON

WAKEFIELD
Birthplace 1732

Ohio River Journey 1770

VA.

YORKTOWN

LOUISIANA
(Spanish)

KENTUCKY
15th State 1792

TENNESSEE
16th State 1796

N.C.

S.C.

Tour of South 1791

GA.

Neutrality Proclamation
During Anglo-French Hostilities
1793

FLORIDA
(Spanish)

John Adams

John Adams is sometimes called the unhappiest president. He was an unpopular victim of turbulent events both at home and abroad. Like Washington's, his politics were conservative and were in strict agreement with the Constitution. In many of his public addresses he spoke of his deep attachment to the great document on which our government is based.

". . . I have repeatedly laid myself under the most serious obligations to support the Constitution," said Adams. "The operation of it has equaled the most sanguine expectations of its friends, and from an habitual attention to it, satisfaction in its administration, and delight in its effects upon the peace, order, prosperity, and happiness of the nation I have acquired an habitual attachment to it and veneration for it. *What other form of government, indeed, can so well deserve our esteem and love?*"

Adams began life on a farm near Braintree, Massachusetts, October 30, 1735. Although he originally wanted to be a minister, he decided "for financial reasons" to study law. He earned money for his

training by teaching school. John Adams graduated from Harvard College at the age of nineteen. This was in 1755. Three years later, he was admitted to the bar. He married Abigail Smith in 1764.

Adams' defense of British soldiers on trial for shooting citizens in the Boston Massacre and his resolutions opposing the Stamp Act brought him prominence. His political convictions were strong. He was glad to serve on the committee to draft the Declaration of Independence and happy to sign his name to that explosive document. John Adams served the new American government as a diplomat, staying in Europe ten years. He helped Benjamin Franklin and John Jay negotiate the peace treaty with Britain in 1783. Afterward, he remained as minister to England from 1785 to 1788.

Adams was called home in June 1788, and soon took up the duties of vice-president in Washington's administration. He assumed that he would become president upon Washington's retirement. Instead, through the political scheming of Hamilton, he nearly lost the election in 1796. He gained the presidency by receiving only three more electoral votes than Thomas Jefferson, who was elected vice-president.

Adams was apprehensive and bitter as he took office on the blustery, gray day of March 4, 1797. He delivered his inaugural address with George Washington seated in the audience. His words sounded defensive. As later events were to prove, he had little

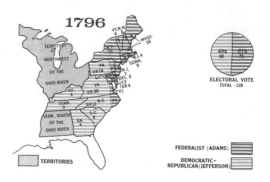

1796

ELECTORAL VOTE
TOTAL -139

TERRITORIES

FEDERALIST (ADAMS)
DEMOCRATIC-
REPUBLICAN (JEFFERSON)

support from the people or from his political associates. The infant nation was rallying for war with the slogan, "Millions for defense, but not one cent for tribute," as France plotted to get England quarreling with her former colonies. Yet Adams stood firm and signed a highly unpopular treaty with France — an act which hurt him politically, but which may well have saved the nation from destruction at that moment.

A census in 1800 showed a population of 5,308,483. This was the year that Spain ceded the Louisiana Territory to France, and Napoleon was warring with England, Austria, and Russia. The passage of the unpopular Alien and Sedition Acts hastened the end of Adams' Federalist Party. These acts had been planned by the Federalists to stop criticism of the American government, especially criticism by French citizens living in the United States. Under the new laws, such criticism became a criminal offense. Americans, whose pride in their Bill of Rights burned fiercely, protested loudly. Actually, Adams had little to do with the Acts; he made no attempt to enforce them. Still, their association with his party· seriously damaged his political future.

The construction of the White House was begun in 1792, but not until November 1800 did President and Mrs. Adams go to live in the mansion which was still unfinished. Earlier that year, Congress moved from Philadelphia to the muddy capital city of Washington.

A close vote kept John Adams from serving a second term as president. He received sixty-five votes while Thomas Jefferson and Aaron Burr each received seventy-three votes. The House of Representatives chose Jefferson. Adams, deeply disappointed, retired to his Massachusetts home without waiting to witness Jefferson's inauguration. But his bitterness lessened in the quiet of retirement. He renewed his old friendship with Thomas Jefferson and maintained correspondence with him for many years.

John Adams lived to see his son John Quincy Adams enter the White House in 1825. He died July 4, 1826, in Quincy, Massachusetts, at the age of ninety.

Thomas Jefferson

Thomas Jefferson was architect, lawyer, inventor, author, musician, and statesman. He was probably the most versatile and talented of American presidents. His ideas were often considered radical in his day, yet he was a consistent champion of liberty and of representative government. The "liberal" Democrats of the 1960's claim him as their party founder, just as Lincoln is claimed by the Republicans. Yet Jefferson strongly believed in limited federal power and in strict governmental economy, which are two basic political viewpoints of the modern "conservatives."

Born April 13, 1743, on a farm in Albemarle County, Virginia, Jefferson stemmed from the proud Tidewater aristocrats who produced America's greatest early leaders. His father, Peter Jefferson, was a surveyor, sheriff, colonel of militia, and a member of the House of Burgesses, while his mother, Jane Randolph Jefferson, was descended from one of Virginia's oldest families.

Young Jefferson entered William and Mary College at Williamsburg at the age of seventeen. He studied law with Judge George Wythe and was admitted to the bar in 1767.

It is evident that he was always driven by a lively curiosity and an intense interest in almost every subject or field of endeavor. He personally designed his beautiful home, Monticello, and during his lifetime filled this mansion with a variety of amazing devices of his own invention. A revolving swivel chair, ingenious locks, and dumb-waiters which he designed are still on view at this historic homestead. Jefferson can be thanked by Americans for the decimal money system — the simplest, and easiest to use system among the world's leading nations to this day.

Strangely, he was not an eloquent speaker. It was his ability to write that brought him most of his political success.

While serving in the Virginia House of Burgesses he was active in organizing action committees against Britain. Chosen to represent Albemarle County at the Virginia conventions, he was sent as a delegate to the Second Continental Congress. There

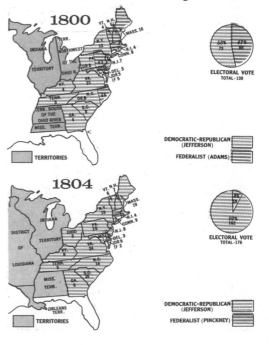

he soon found himself on a committee to draft a Declaration of Independence with John Adams, Benjamin Franklin, Roger Sherman, and Robert Livingston. He wrote the first draft which was approved by the committee as well as by the Congress with only a few changes.

Jefferson returned to Virginia and was elected governor during the Revolution. He held this office in 1779 and 1780. It was during this period that he fled to escape capture by British troops. Roundly criticized by his political opponents, he resigned as governor. Shortly afterward, his wife, the former Martha Wayles Skelton, died in September 1782. For several months Jefferson was so despondent that he had almost no contact with friends or relatives.

However, when he was elected to Congress in 1783 he began a vigorous new phase of his life. George Washington appointed him secretary of state, and he served as vice-president under John Adams. The election of 1800 nearly wrecked the government, as Jefferson and Aaron Burr each received seventy-three electoral votes. This stalemate was finally broken by a vote in the House of Representatives. This group voted in favor of Jefferson.

Thomas Jefferson was the first president to be inaugurated in Washington, D.C. He walked along muddy Pennsylvania Avenue to deliver his address at the unfinished Capitol. In this surprisingly mild speech, he said, "Sometimes it is said that man cannot be trusted with the government of himself. Can he, then, be trusted with the government of others? Or have we found angels in the forms of kings to govern him?"

Jefferson's handling of the war with Tripoli, his daring purchase of the Louisiana Territory from France in 1803 for approximately fifteen million dollars, and the rising prosperity of the country, all helped to win him reelection in 1804 by an overwhelming 162 electoral votes.

In 1809 he retired to Monticello, where for seventeen years he pursued his many interests. Jefferson died July 4, 1826, the same day as John Adams' death.

James Madison

Mar. 4,
1809
-
Mar. 3,
1817

A procession of Virginia statesmen continued to fill the major offices of the growing United States government. James Madison, the fourth president, was another Virginia plantation owner's son. Born March 16, 1751, at Port Conway, Va., he was a frail and sickly child; he remained short and slight throughout his life. Yet his political stature as one of the founders of the nation rivaled Washington's and Jefferson's. He was the "master builder of the Constitution." It was Madison who conceived the plan for the House of Representatives, with its power of taxation, and he helped to create the checks and balances in other branches of government in order to prevent concentration of power.

James was a brilliant student. He could read Greek, Latin, and Spanish at the age of twelve. He graduated from Princeton University in 1771.

He was physically unfit for military service, so he became active in politics at the beginning of the American Revolution. He sat in the Virginia assembly at the age of twenty-five. He helped to draft a new con

stitution for Virginia. This document later became the model for other colonies. In 1778, he became a member of the governor's council; then, a year later, he won election as a Virginia representative to the Continental Congress.

When Madison returned home in 1783, he was firmly established as a political leader. Following the war he played an active part in the drafting of the Constitution and in getting it ratified by his home state of Virginia. He was the chief author of the first ten amendments to the Constitution, known as the Bill of Rights.

Over the years a strong bond of friendship and of political agreement grew up between Thomas Jefferson and James Madison. Madison served as Jefferson's secretary of state, then was picked by Jefferson to be his successor to the presidency. Madison won this election easily, receiving 122 electoral votes against 47 for Federalist C. C. Pinckney. Riding stylishly in a coach to deliver his first inaugural address at the Capitol, on March

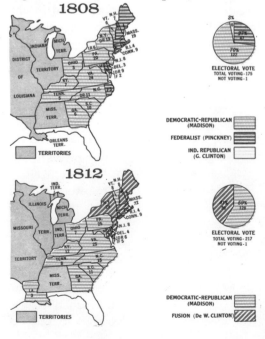

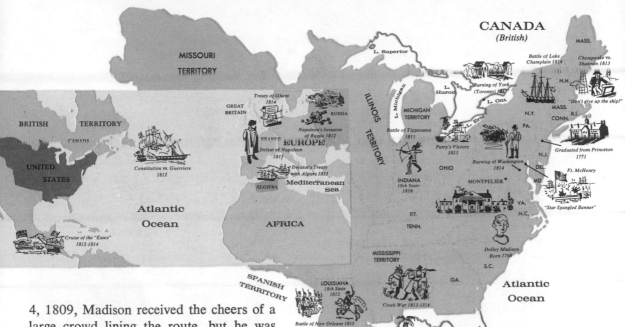

The map shows the United States and surrounding regions during the Madison era with labeled illustrations including: CANADA (British), MASS., MISSOURI TERRITORY, Battle of Lake Champlain 1814, Chesapeake vs. Shannon 1813, BRITISH TERRITORY, CANADA, UNITED STATES, GREAT BRITAIN, Treaty of Ghent 1814, RUSSIA, Napoleon's Invasion of Russia 1812, ILLINOIS TERRITORY, L. Superior, L. Huron, L. Michigan, L. Ont., L. Erie, N.H., MASS., N.Y., PA., CONN., R.I., Burning of York (Toronto) 1813, "Don't give up the ship!", MICHIGAN TERRITORY, Battle of Tippecanoe 1811, Perry's Victory 1813, N.J., DEL., Graduated from Princeton 1771, FRANCE, EUROPE, Defeat of Napoleon 1815, Decatur's Treaty with Algiers 1815, ALGIERS, Mediterranean Sea, Constitution vs. Guerriere 1812, Atlantic Ocean, AFRICA, INDIANA 19th State 1816, OHIO, Burning of Washington 1814, MONTPELIER, MD., VA., Ft. McHenry, "Star Spangled Banner", KY., TENN., N.C., Dolley Madison Born 1768, S.C., Cruise of the "Essex" 1812-1814, MISSISSIPPI TERRITORY, GA., Atlantic Ocean, SPANISH TERRITORY, LOUISIANA 18th State 1812, Creek War 1813-1814, Battle of New Orleans 1815, Annexation of West Florida 1810, FLORIDA (Spanish), Gulf of Mexico.

4, 1809, Madison received the cheers of a large crowd lining the route, but he was aware that much of the enthusiasm was for Thomas Jefferson who was riding behind the coach. This did not embarrass Madison and in his inaugural address he clearly set forth a restatement of Jefferson's policies.

As Madison entered the White House, however, a new pattern was set for Washington social life. The charming Dolley Madison — the former Dolley Payne Todd, whom James had married in 1794 — became the hostess of many brilliant White House entertainments. She became known for her well-managed banquets and for serving unusual dishes. Ice cream appeared at White House dinner parties for the first time during the Madisons' occupancy.

Madison's term began at a time when the population of the United States was 7,239,881. This represented an increase of about 2,000,000 persons in ten years. The nation was growing rapidly and flexing its young muscles. In 1811, General William Henry Harrison stamped out a British-supported Indian uprising in Indiana Territory at the battle of Tippecanoe Creek.

Meanwhile, trouble abroad made Madison's first term an uncomfortable one. The War of 1812 was blamed upon the President although he entered it reluctantly. In spite of growing criticism, Madison was

reelected, and delivered his second inaugural address March 4, 1813. In this speech he defended his war policies and attempted to paint an optimistic picture of final victory. Nevertheless, only a few months later, Madison and his wife were forced to flee Washington when the British sacked and burned the Capitol and the White House. Dolley Madison is credited with rescuing the Declaration of Independence and a valuable portrait of Washington during a hair-raising, last-minute escape.

Andrew Jackson's victory at New Orleans, in 1815, helped to bring the unpopular war to a close. This made it possible for Madison to retire under favorable conditions. He returned to his beautiful estate, Montpelier, in Orange County, Virginia, where he spent a number of happy years managing his property. In 1826, he became rector (now called president) of the University of Virginia.

The smallest president and greatest architect of the United States Constitutional Government died at Montpelier, Va., June 28, 1836, at the age of eighty-five.

James Monroe

By the time James Monroe became the fifth president, the United States of America had undergone a baptism of fire, and a truly great and powerful nation was beginning to take form. Despite the sacking and burning of Washington, D.C., the United States emerged victorious in Andrew Jackson's stunning defeat of the British at New Orleans. In 1815, Captain Stephen Decatur permanently crushed the Barbary pirates. The world's navies began to eye American ships with respect.

Throughout this colorful period of U.S. history, a shy, somewhat arrogant Virginian had been playing an important political role. His name was James Monroe. He was born in George Washington's Westmoreland County, April 28, 1758, and entered the political scene at an early age. After distinguishing himself as a youthful officer at the battles of White Plains, Monmouth, Brandywine, Germantown, and Trenton, he was elected to the Virginia assembly in 1782. He was only twenty-four at the time. Shortly afterward, he served three years in the Continental Congress. His political ideas were influenced by Thomas Jefferson, under whom Monroe had studied law. He was opposed to a strong centralized government, and he was not enthusiastic about the Constitution, although he finally voted for its ratification by his home state of Virginia. During a term as U.S. Senator, Monroe took sides with Jefferson and Madison against Hamilton's Federalist policies. These three great Virginians are credited with founding the Democratic-Republican Party.

Although Monroe's diplomatic career nearly collapsed a number of times, his prestige somehow survived. As minister to France, he angered President Washington by criticising a treaty with Britain. Again, as a minister to Great Britain for Thomas Jefferson, he negotiated a trade treaty that was unacceptable and was never submitted to the Senate. Yet it was Monroe who helped Robert Livingston conclude the Louisiana Purchase, one of the great master strokes in the history of international

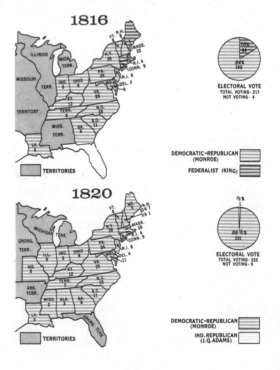

1816

ELECTORAL VOTE
TOTAL VOTING - 217
NOT VOTING - 4

DEMOCRATIC-REPUBLICAN
(MONROE)
FEDERALIST (KING)

TERRITORIES

1820

ELECTORAL VOTE
TOTAL VOTING - 232
NOT VOTING - 3

DEMOCRATIC-REPUBLICAN
(MONROE)
IND. REPUBLICAN
(J.Q. ADAMS)

TERRITORIES

diplomacy. Afterward, he was elected governor of Virginia, was appointed secretary of state by Madison, and at the same time filled the post of secretary of war when John Armstrong was dismissed.

James Monroe was elected president while still serving as secretary of state. His two inaugural addresses, 1817 and 1821, reflected a jubilant reaction to his overwhelming victories. For his second term he was unopposed, thus becoming the only president other than George Washington to be the sole candidate in an election. Yet he did not receive a unanimous vote in the electoral college since one elector voted for John Quincy Adams.

During Monroe's administration, the nation grew and prospered. Five new states were added: Mississippi, Illinois, Alabama, Maine, Missouri. It was in this period, when the Central American countries separated from Spain and Brazil broke away from Portugal, that Monroe proclaimed his famous "hands-off" doctrine, guaranteeing protection of the Americas against European interference. This statement was called the Monroe Doctrine. It became a basic policy of U.S. international relations.

During his presidency, Monroe's concepts of government gradually shifted toward Federalist ideas of stronger central power. The nation was expanding so rapidly that the President had to exercise greater controls in order to hold the Union together. His administration, known as "the era of good feeling," was an era of national successes and increasing prosperity, but the seeds of sectional conflict had been sown. The shadow of civil war was cast by the quarrel over the admission of Missouri as a slaveholding state. After bitter argument in Congress, an agreement was made to admit Maine as a free state and Missouri as a slaveholding state. This agreement, called the Missouri Compromise, also prohibited slavery in any state made from the Louisiana Purchase lands north of Missouri's southern boundary. The President took neither side in the dispute, but gave his approval to the compromise bill.

Monroe retired to his Oak Hill estate near Leesburg, Va., and served for five years as a regent of the University of Virginia. Later he presided at the Virginia Constitutional Convention. He died in New York City, July 4, 1831.

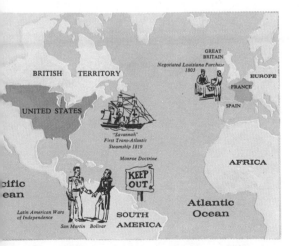

John Quincy Adams

History does not always provide ideal circumstances for her great leaders. John Quincy Adams was one of the most remarkable personalities among the American presidents, yet his term of office was marked with bitterness and frustration. To begin with, he was elected by Congress, after the members of the electoral college had awarded him less votes than Andrew Jackson. There were four candidates. Adams received eighty-four votes to Jackson's ninety-nine. William H. Crawford received forty-one votes, and Henry Clay, thirty-seven. None of the four could be elected without a majority of the total votes cast. Congress, therefore, was called upon to select one of the first three, and Henry Clay, in last place, threw his support to Adams. For the remainder of his life, Adams suffered the stigma of a "deal" between himself and Clay, particularly after he appointed Clay his secretary of state.

But John Quincy Adams, the only son of a president to become president, was a man of such political honesty that he lost popularity largely because he refused to vote or act along party lines. It is doubtful that he was guilty of any secret understanding with Clay.

John Quincy Adams was born July 11, 1767, in Braintree (now Quincy), Mass. He was exposed to politics and diplomacy at a very early age. When he was ten years old, he accompanied his father on the dangerous voyage to France. While the elder Adams carried out his diplomatic assignments, young John attended schools in Paris, Amsterdam and Leyden. He was only fourteen when he traveled to St. Petersburg, Russia, as private secretary to Francis Dana, America's first ambassador to Russia.

In 1785, he entered Harvard College and graduated in 1787. Although he was admitted to the bar in 1790, he did not have much success as a lawyer. However, a series of newspaper articles on political subjects brought him national attention. At the age of twenty-seven he was appointed Washington's minister to the Netherlands. While his father, John Adams, was president, he served as minister to Prussia. Later he was elected to the Massachusetts Senate, then to the U.S. Senate. He was minister to Russia, minister to England, and finally became secretary of state in Monroe's cabinet. In this office, he made an agreement with Britain for both countries to occupy the Oregon territory,

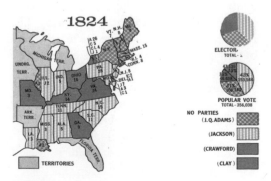

1824

ELECTOR.
TOTAL - 2

POPULAR VOTE
TOTAL - 356,038

NO PARTIES
(J.Q.ADAMS)

(JACKSON)

(CRAWFORD)

(CLAY)

TERRITORIES

and he purchased Florida from Spain.

As president, John Quincy Adams recommended some federal projects which included the construction of highways and canals, weather stations, public buildings, and the establishment of a national university. But the opposition of Jackson's followers was so strong that this progressive program was blocked. After four years as president, John Quincy Adams was defeated in his bid for reelection. The popular Andrew Jackson, hero of New Orleans and the Florida campaign, overwhelmed him in the 1828 election.

Adams returned to Massachusetts sorely disappointed and embittered. But some of his greatest work still lay ahead of him. He was persuaded to run for Congress in 1830, and he defeated two opponents by a large majority. For seventeen years he served in the House of Representatives, and remained one of the nation's leading figures. He became chairman of the House Foreign Affairs Committee, and he successfully fought the efforts of Southern congressmen to prevent the reading of petitions to end slavery. These "gag rules," as they were called, were finally abolished, mostly because of the work of Adams. He opposed many of Andrew Jackson's policies, espe-

cially that of recognizing the independence of Texas. However, he firmly supported "Old Hickory's" foreign policy, thus showing again his remarkable moral and political honesty.

Adams was active to the end of his life. He was an untiring opponent of slavery. While at work in Washington, D.C., he suffered two paralytic strokes. His second attack came while he was at his desk in the House of Representatives. He was carried to the speaker's office and he died in that room two days later. The date was February 23, 1848.

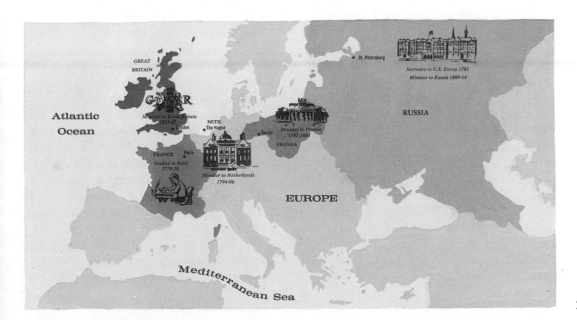

Andrew Jackson

The name "Old Hickory" conjures up an image of the tough, vigorous frontier America that we view today with wistful admiration. Andrew Jackson's life story reads like the most robust of adventure novels.

He was born in a log cabin March 15, 1767. The exact location of Andrew's birthplace is not known, although it is generally believed to be near the border town of Waxhaw, N.C. Jackson was the son of poor farm folk who came to the Carolina frontier from Northern Ireland. Young Andrew's Irish temper led him into many a boyhood fight, and it influenced his actions throughout his turbulent life.

After brief schooling in the Waxhaw Presbyterian Church and in a nearby boarding school, he joined the Revolutionary militia at the age of fourteen. He was captured by a British raiding party in 1781. When one of the British officers ordered Andrew to polish his boots, the boy refused. The officer struck him with his sword, cutting his hand to the bone and gashing his head deeply. Andrew Jackson carried these scars for life. A few years later he persuaded a wealthy lawyer in Salisbury, N.C., Spruce Macay, to teach him law. He was admitted to the bar in 1787, when he was twenty years old and still too young to vote! Jackson achieved considerable success practicing law and was appointed attorney general for the lawless North Carolina frontier — a region which later became the state of Tennessee. Then, in 1796, he was elected to the House of Representatives by this new state.

Jackson finally found an outlet for his fighting temper with the outbreak of the War of 1812. He quickly offered his services to President Madison. On a five-hundred-mile march through the wilderness, General Jackson walked so that his horse could carry a wounded soldier. His men urged him to ride but he refused. One of the soldiers said, "He's tough — tough as a hickory!" The nickname, "Old Hickory," stuck with him. Jackson attacked and annihilated a large force of Creek Indians, was elevated to major general in the regular army, captured Pensacola in Florida, and went on to New Orleans. There, with five thousand men he routed eight thousand British. Enemy losses were over two thousand contrasted with the American loss of less than twenty killed and wounded.

Old Hickory was now a national hero. Soon he was persuaded by friends and by newspapers in Nashville to run for the presidency. But though he won more electoral votes than any of the three other candidates in the 1824 election, Congress chose John Quincy Adams. Immediately, angry Jackson supporters declared political war on President Adams. Four years later, Jackson won by a wide margin. He stood on the Capitol steps to deliver his first inaugural address. He was happy because of this long sought victory, but

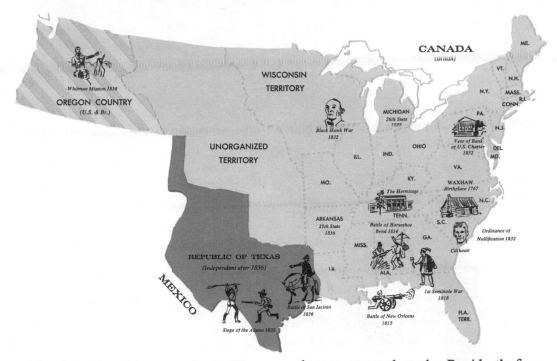

CANADA
(British)

OREGON COUNTRY
(U.S. & Br.)

Whitman Mission 1836

WISCONSIN TERRITORY

UNORGANIZED TERRITORY

ME.
VT.
N.H.
N.Y.
MASS.
R.I.
CONN.
PA.
N.J.
DEL.
MD.
VA.

Black Hawk War 1832

MICHIGAN
26th State
1837

OHIO

ILL.
IND.

Veto of Bank of U.S. Charter 1832

MO.

KY.

The Hermitage

ARKANSAS
25th State
1836

TENN.

Battle of Horseshoe Bend 1814

MISS.

GA.

S.C.

N.C.

WAXHAW
Birthplace 1767

Ordinance of Nullification 1832

Calhoun

REPUBLIC OF TEXAS
(Independent after 1836)

MEXICO

Battle of San Jacinto 1836

LA.

ALA.

1st Seminole War 1818

FLA. TERR.

Siege of the Alamo 1836

Battle of New Orleans 1815

saddened by his wife's recent death. Here was, perhaps, the first true "man of the people" to direct the nation's destiny, and his philosophy was plain and direct. It was natural that tough Old Hickory should believe in a strong central government, but Vice-President Calhoun, a "state's righter," believed in a strong state government. President Jackson appointed many of his supporters to important posts. This was to be expected of a man who was fiercely loyal to his friends and quick to anger with his enemies.

During his eight-year administration, Jackson vetoed a bill which would have renewed the charter of The Bank of the United States. Vice-President John C. Calhoun resigned, and a number of cabinet changes occurred as the President's fiery temper continued to flare. He pressed strongly for western expansion, succeeded in persuading Britain to allow American ships trading rights in the West Indies. He was faced with one of the first serious secession crises when South Carolina refused to abide by tariff laws passed by Congress. After Jackson had threatened force and Congress had passed a compromise tariff bill, the crisis eased.

Jackson retired to his home, the Hermitage. Although he was a sick man, he supervised management of this plantation for several years. On June 8, 1845, he died, surrounded by his grieving slaves. Old Hickory had been tough as hickory and straight as an arrow to the end.

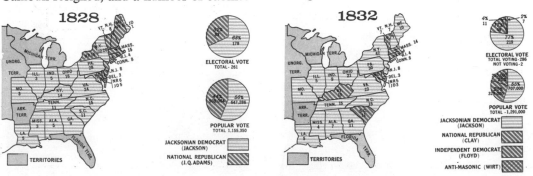

1828

MICHIGAN TERR.
UNORG. TERR.
VT. N.H. ME.
N.Y.
MASS. 15
R.I. 4
CONN. 8
PA. 28
N.J. 8
DEL. 3
INR 6
J D 5
ILL. 3
IND. 5
OHIO 16
MO. 3
KY. 14
VA. 24
N.C. 15
TENN. 11
ARK. TERR.
MISS. 3
ALA. 5
GA. 9
S.C. 11
LA. 5
FLORIDA TERR.

TERRITORIES

ELECTORAL VOTE
TOTAL - 261

68%
178

POPULAR VOTE
TOTAL 1,155,350

66%
647,286

JACKSONIAN DEMOCRAT
(JACKSON)

NATIONAL REPUBLICAN
(J.Q. ADAMS)

1832

MICHIGAN TERR.
UNORG. TERR.
VT. N.H. ME.
7 7 10
N.Y.
MASS. 14
R.I. 4
CONN. 8
PA. 30
N.J. 8
DEL. 3
INR 5
J D 3
ILL. 5
IND. 9
OHIO 21
MO. 4
KY.
VA. 23
N.C. 15
TENN. 15
ARK. TERR.
MISS. 4
ALA. 7
GA. 11
LA. 5
FLORIDA TERR.

TERRITORIES

ELECTORAL VOTE
TOTAL VOTING-286
NOT VOTING-2

4%
11
2%
7
77%
219

POPULAR VOTE
TOTAL - 1,291,000

55%
707,000

JACKSONIAN DEMOCRAT
(JACKSON)

NATIONAL REPUBLICAN
(CLAY)

INDEPENDENT DEMOCRAT
(FLOYD)

ANTI-MASONIC (WIRT)

Martin Van Buren

The little Dutch community of Kinderhook, New York, was the birthplace of Martin Van Buren, who was destined to become the eighth President of the United States. Martin was born December 5, 1782, the third of five children and the son of Abraham and Maria Hoes Van Buren. After attending the local country school and Kinderhook Academy, he showed his desire to be a lawyer at a very early age. He was only fourteen when he became an office boy in a local law firm, where attorney Francis Sylvester gave him his early instruction. In 1799, when he was seventeen, he borrowed forty dollars and went to New York City. There, he became a clerk in a law office, completed his studies and was admitted to the bar in 1803.

Van Buren, slight and dapper, was fond of stylish dress, social life, and fine carriages. He rode to his inauguration in a handsome phaeton that had been constructed of timbers from the frigate *Old Ironsides*. Friends nicknamed him "The Little Magician," and as an astute lawyer and clever politician he had earned the title.

Van Buren moved rapidly into the political arena, beginning with his attendance at a political convention at the age of twenty. He was a county surrogate at twenty-five, state senator in 1812, and New York Attorney General in 1816. Finally, he won election to the U.S. Senate in 1821. There he plunged directly into the hottest issues of the day, leading a fight to abolish debtor's prison and succeeding in getting the law passed in 1828. From the beginning he was outspoken against slavery.

"The Little Magician's" next post was governor of New York, which he won in 1828. He had supported Andrew Jackson's bid for the presidency, and was rewarded, after serving as governor for only a few weeks, by appointment as Jackson's secretary of state. From this point, Jackson's well-known loyalty carried Van Buren to the heights. Jackson appointed him minister to Great Britain, but the Senate failed to confirm the appointment by one vote. In spite of this, Jackson chose Van Buren as his vice-president in 1832, and carried his running mate into office with a resounding victory. Van Buren returned these favors by supporting Jackson's unpopular policies toward the Bank of the United States. When his life was threatened by angry political enemies, Van Buren carried loaded pistols into the Senate chamber and kept his weapons with him while he presided over the Senate.

By this time, Jackson had made it clear

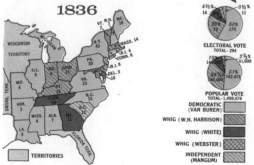

that he expected Martin Van Buren to be his successor. With Jackson's wholehearted support, Van Buren won the 1836 election with 170 electoral votes and 762,678 popular votes, against William Henry Harrison's 73 electoral and 549,000 popular votes.

Van Buren took office riding the crest of his successful wave and delivered an address that glittered with optimism. The country had just witnessed Samuel Morse's invention of the telegraph. General Sam Houston had avenged the Alamo by defeating Santa Anna at the Battle of San Jacinto River. And the Liberty Bell had been cracked, tolling the death of Chief Justice John Marshall in 1835. But though western expansion was still booming, a deep financial depression occurred only thirty-six days after Van Buren's administration began. Almost all banks in the country closed their doors while hundreds of them failed. This was due mainly to the Jackson policies regarding money, which Van Buren had supported.

The result for the President was a rapid loss of popularity. Depression, slavery problems, his opposition to the annexation of Texas, all contributed to Van Buren's political backsliding. He was renominated in 1840, but William Henry Harrison's Whig Party whooped up a boisterous campaign and won by a surprisingly close popular vote.

Van Buren returned to his country estate, Lindenwald, in his native town of Kinderhook. For another twenty years he remained active in politics. The Free Soil Party nominated him for the presidency in 1848, but he was defeated, although he polled a large New York State vote. He was a strong antislavery supporter, yet as a loyal Democrat he opposed Lincoln in 1860, only to throw his full support to the Civil War President after the election. He died at his estate July 24, 1862.

Despite a troublesome term, Van Buren never lost optimism for America's future. His words were prophetic: ". . . America will present to every friend of mankind the cheering proof that a popular government, wisely formed, is wanting in no element of endurance or strength."

27

William Henry Harrison

Military heroes have occupied the White House many times, and one of the most colorful of such figures was William Henry Harrison, victor in the bloody battle with Indian forces at Tippecanoe Creek in Indiana. Whether or not Harrison would have been a good president will never be known, for he served the shortest term in the history of U.S. presidents. The indications are that, while he was an excellent military leader and an honest administrator, he would have made a poor showing as president, partly because he was elected by a party whose leaders wanted him only as a figurehead. There is evidence, too, that the wild campaign which his Whig Party conducted turned his head and inflated his opinion of himself to dangerous proportions.

Harrison was born February 9, 1773, on the family plantation, Berkeley, in Charles City County, Virginia. His father, Benjamin Harrison, who had served in the two Continental Congresses, was a signer of the Declaration of Independence. William received his early education by being tutored at home. Although he attended Hampden-

Sydney College for a short time, he left before graduation and joined the army in 1791. He served in Ohio Indian wars under "Mad Anthony" Wayne. This was in 1794. A short time afterward he was promoted to captain and placed in command of Fort Washington, Ohio. There he met and married Anna Symmes.

When President John Adams appointed Harrison secretary of Northwest Territory, the young soldier resigned his Army commission. At the age of twenty-six, he was elected by settlers as the Territory's first delegate to Congress. A year later Adams asked him to take over the governorship of Indiana Territory. This proved to be the outstanding period of his career. In the vast Indian country stretching from the Ohio River to the Rocky Mountains, Harrison made sincere efforts to help the Indians and to promote their welfare. One of his first acts as governor was to ban the sale of liquor to Indians. He gave them medical assistance, innoculated them against smallpox, and offered them educational opportunities. As a result of these policies, he was able to negotiate a treaty with chiefs of the major tribes. This treaty awarded some two and one-half million acres of territory to white settlers along the Wabash and White Rivers. But a large number of renegade Indians joined forces with the chief of the Shawnees, Tecumseh,

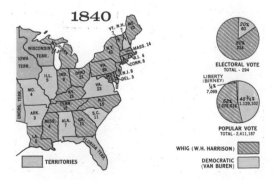

and his brother The Prophet to fight American encroachment on their lands.

Harrison saw that firm action would have to be taken in order to make the treaty stick. He organized a force of militia, led them against the rebellious Indians, and on November 7, 1811, he met and smashed a superior force at Tippecanoe Creek. From that day, Harrison bore the popular nickname of "Old Tippecanoe."

With the outbreak of the War of 1812, President Madison placed Harrison in command of the Army of the Northwest. Old Tippecanoe won a spectacular victory when he defeated Indians and British soldiers in southern Ontario at the Battle of the Thames.

After the war, Harrison's political career resumed with his election in 1816 to the U.S. House of Representatives. He became a senator from Ohio in 1825. A brief sojourn as minister to Colombia ended when he angered Simon Bolivar by telling him not to set himself up as a dictator.

Harrison's first bid for the presidency failed in 1836. But four years later the Whigs renominated him and chose John Tyler for the vice-presidential running mate. In one of the most uproarious election campaigns in U.S. history, the Whigs, with no platform or special political philosophy, ballyhooed their way to victory with the famous slogan, "Tippecanoe and Tyler too." Harrison won by 234 electoral votes to Van Buren's 60. He rode hatless on a white horse to deliver his inaugural address, though the day was cold and rainy. This attempt to assume the pose of a tough, masterful leader probably cost Harrison his life. After assigning Daniel Webster the task of settling a dispute with Great Britain during the first week of his administration, Harrison caught a fresh cold. His cold developed into pneumonia, and he died April 4, 1841, a brief thirty days after becoming President of the United States.

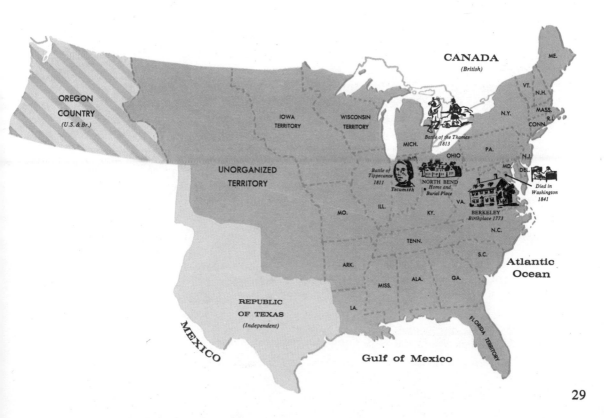

John Tyler

One of the most vilified and unpopular of American presidents was John Tyler, the first man to assume the high office upon the death of a Chief Executive. Yet looking at his four-year term in the perspective of time, it is apparent that in many respects he was a stronger and a better executive than Harrison would have been. He demonstrated unusual courage in the face of strenuous opposition, and he made some worthwhile accomplishments in spite of his difficult situation.

Another native of Virginia, Tyler was born on his father's Greenways Estate, located in Charles City County. He was a headstrong lad, and the story is told that he once led a rebellion of pupils against a hated schoolmaster. In 1802 he entered William and Mary College, where he showed an early interest in political science and law. But he had visions of being a musician, and he became an accomplished violinist. The law won out, however, when he began studying with his father, a distinguished judge. Young Tyler was admitted to the bar in 1809. This was merely a beginning to a political career, for he won an election to the Virginia legislature two years later, at the age of twenty-one.

This tall, slender, blue-eyed man won the confidence of his constituents by a calm dignity and patience that marked his entire career. He was elected to the House of Representatives in 1816; he was then twenty-six years old. As a congressman, he fought constantly for strict adherence to the Constitution and against any extension of federal power. For example, he opposed John C. Calhoun's program of federal projects for improved roads and canals, and supported Jackson in his condemnation of the Bank of the United States. On the other hand, he took the side of Calhoun in the matter of nullification and states' rights, when Calhoun proposed that states should

have the right to declare acts of Congress null and void.

At the age of thirty-five John Tyler became governor of Virginia. Two years later, he was back in Congress, this time as senator. But he found himself trapped by his own political consistency. Though he agreed with Jackson's negative view of the Bank of the United States, he felt that the president had no right to withdraw government funds on his own initiative. Tyler therefore refused to abide by instructions from the Virginia legislature who wanted him to vote away the Senate-imposed censure of Jackson's policies. Called "Turncoat Tyler" by Jackson Democrats, he resigned from the Senate and aligned himself with the Whig Party.

Tyler found himself increasingly a politician without a party because of his refusal to compromise his own principles. Probably the Whigs would have abandoned him had they not needed a vice-presidential candidate who, they felt, would appeal to Southern "states' righters." This was the reason "Tippecanoe and Tyler too" became

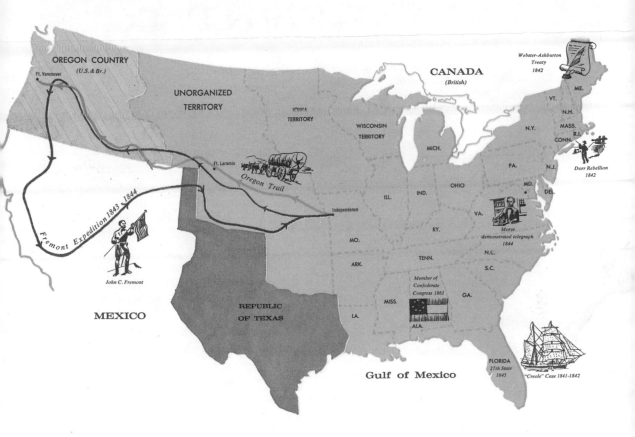

the 1840 Whig ticket. Tyler was elected with Harrison, then fate plummeted him into the presidency upon the old war hero's unexpected death.

It is said that Tyler was playing a game of marbles with his sons in Williamsburg when he learned of Harrison's death. No sooner was he sworn in at the Capitol than his political enemies branded him "Acting President." Tyler took it in stride. When Henry Clay pushed a number of bills through Congress, calling for establishment of a new United States Bank and higher tariffs, Tyler promptly vetoed them, one after another. Outraged mobs marched on the White House, hurling rocks and insults. Tyler was not afraid. He calmly armed the White House servants and waited for the crowd to disperse.

Tyler was burned in effigy. He was the first president to have impeachment proceedings introduced by Congressional leaders. The effort failed.

Meanwhile, Tyler signed into law the Pre-emption Act of 1841 awarding a settler 160 acres of public land if he built a cabin on the property. At the end of his term, he signed a resolution admitting Texas and a bill admitting Florida to the Union.

The tenth president retired to Charles City, Va., where he lived quietly until 1861 when he acted as chairman of a peace conference attempting to avoid civil war. Later he served in the provisional Congress of the Confederate States. When Tyler died on January 18, 1862, the government took no official notice of his death. In 1911, Congress authorized a monument in his honor. It was completed in 1915 and dedicated later that year.

James Knox Polk

In this day of political campaign promises, it is hard to imagine a president who really means what he says, and whose sole object is to get a job done in the manner he thinks it should be done. Yet such a man was James Polk, a "dark horse" candidate, who made comparatively little effort to become president, refused to run for a second term, and almost killed himself with four years of hard work.

Polk's father was a farmer in ordinary circumstances. He had a modest farm, but he wanted his son to have a good education. James was born November 2, 1795, at Little Sugar Creek near Pineville in North Carolina. The family moved to Tennessee when James was still a boy. As he wanted to become a teacher, he did a great deal of reading, attempting to educate himself. In 1815, his father sent him to the University of North Carolina. He graduated at the top of his class, and delivered a graduation address in Latin.

Curiously, this restrained, scholarly man —entirely different from the fiery tempered Andrew Jackson—became a close personal and political friend of Old Hickory. He made the acquaintance of General Jackson while studying law with Felix Grundy in Nashville. From that time, Polk was such an admirer, supporter, and associate of Jackson's that he earned the nickname of "Young Hickory." After becoming a successful lawyer in Columbia, Tenn., he won election to the Tennessee legislature in 1823. Two years later, at the age of thirty, he was elected to Congress, where for fourteen years he fought vigorously for Southern interests, slavery, and states' rights. When Andrew Jackson became president, Polk supported his policies.

Polk was elected governor of Tennessee in 1839. In that office, he continued to work for states' rights legislation and against concentrated power in Washington. Tennessee society soon learned that Polk and his wife, the former Sarah Childress, had little interest in social affairs. The couple's stiffness and avoidance of parties and entertainments cost Polk popularity. In 1841, he lost his bid for reelection; he lost again in 1843.

Almost unknown nationally, James Polk unexpectedly became America's first "dark horse" presidential candidate in the 1844 campaign. This came about as a result of a convention deadlock over Van Buren, who could not gain support of delegates from the South and West. Polk was nominated as a compromise candidate on the ninth ballot and won a bandwagon victory.

1844

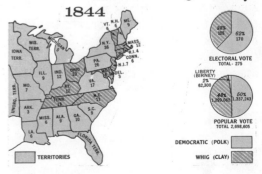

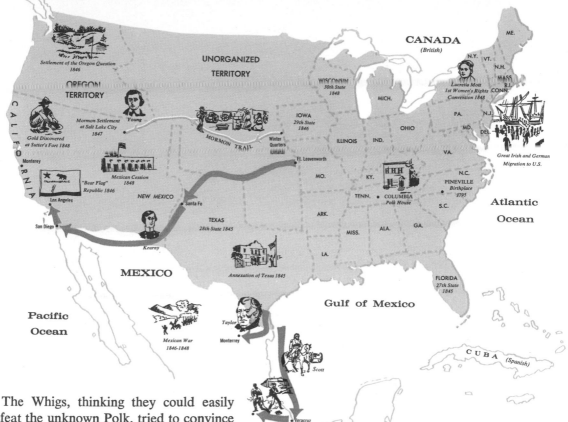

Settlement of the Oregon Question
1846

CANADA
(British)

UNORGANIZED
TERRITORY

OREGON
TERRITORY

Mormon Settlement
at Salt Lake City
1847

Young

WISCONSIN
30th State
1848

MICH.

Lucretia Mott
1st Women's Rights
Convention 1848

ME.

N.Y. VT.
N.H.
MASS.
R.I.
CONN.

Gold Discovered
at Sutter's Fort 1848

CALIFORNIA

MORMON TRAIL

Winter
Quarters
(Omaha)

IOWA
29th State
1846

Ft. Leavenworth

ILLINOIS IND.

OHIO

PA.

N.J.

MD.
DEL.

Great Irish and German
Migration to U.S.

Monterey

Mexican Cession
1848

"Bear Flag"
Republic 1846

NEW MEXICO

Santa Fe

MO.

KY.

VA.

N.C.
PINEVILLE
Birthplace
1795

Los Angeles

COLUMBIA
Polk House

Atlantic
Ocean

San Diego

Kearny

TEXAS
28th State 1845

ARK.

TENN.

S.C.

MEXICO

Annexation of Texas 1845

MISS.

ALA.

GA.

LA.

FLORIDA
27th State
1845

Pacific
Ocean

Taylor

Gulf of Mexico

Mexican War
1846-1848

Monterrey

Scott

CUBA (Spanish)

Veracruz

Fall of Mexico City
1847

The Whigs, thinking they could easily defeat the unknown Polk, tried to convince voters that the Democrat was a political nonentity. But the Democrats stirred the country with the slogan, "54-40 or fight." Thus they played upon the greatest issue of the day, since most Americans wanted to acquire the Oregon Territory north to 54° 40′ latitude, a region occupied jointly by the United States and Great Britain.

Polk won by 170 electoral and 1,337,243 popular votes to Henry Clay's 105 electoral and 1,299,062 popular votes. The eleventh president, James Polk, had stated, prior to his election, that his chief objectives would be to reduce tariffs, settle the dispute over Oregon Territory, acquire California, and restore an independent federal treasury. During his term in office, he accomplished every one of these objectives. He and Mrs. Polk plunged into their task, all business and no frills. Dancing, alcoholic beverages, card playing, elaborate banquets, and Sunday visits were no longer permitted at the White House. Sarah Polk acted as her husband's secretary. He went right to work on the drafting of a new tariff law, which was passed by Congress in 1846. The same year, the Independent Treasury Act set up a national treasury in Washington with depositories in several other major cities.

Meanwhile as the Oregon Trail swarmed with pioneers and settlers, Polk negotiated the Oregon Treaty with Britain, establishing the boundary on the 49th parallel.

To the south, Polk ordered U.S. troops to stand guard along the Rio Grande. Probably he expected to incite an incident. In any case, the Mexicans attacked and Polk asked Congress for a declaration of war. Two years later, the victorious U.S. forces wrung from Mexico a treaty which ceded a vast territory to the United States, including what is now Arizona, California, Colorado, Nevada, New Mexico, Utah, and part of Wyoming. At the same time Mexico abandoned all claims to Texas.

Having worked day and night for four solid years to gain his objectives, Polk retired to his home in Nashville, Tennessee. Three months later he contracted cholera and died June 15, 1849, at age fifty-three.

Zachary Taylor

Perhaps President Polk's Mexican War was not the most savory chapter in American history, yet it had the result of adding vast territories to the United States, and of producing a number of national heroes. Some of these learned military lessons they would find valuable in the Civil War. One of the new heroes was Zachary Taylor, a tough Indian fighter from the Kentucky frontier who had already won the nickname of "Old Rough and Ready."

Taylor had little formal education and few qualifications for the presidency other than indomitable courage and high principle. But these qualities were sufficient to carry him a long way.

Zachary was born November 24, 1784, on a modest farm in Orange County, near Barboursville, Va., the son of a Revolutionary War officer who had fought under Washington and had participated in the Battle of Trenton. As his war bonus, Richard Taylor was awarded six thousand acres of land in Kentucky. He moved his family to this tract, near Louisville, in 1785, only a few months after Zachary was born. Consequently, young Zachary grew up in one of the wildest of the early frontier areas and in the midst of constant Indian warfare. From his earliest days he longed to become a soldier. For a time he was instructed by tutors, and for a short while he attended a country school, but most of his boyhood was spent working on his father's farm. Then, at age twenty-three he was appointed a lieutenant in the army. Two years later Taylor was promoted to captain.

By now, Zachary Taylor was thoroughly committed to an army career. No military genius, he was nevertheless a born leader and a determined fighter. His defense of Fort Harrison, Indiana, in the War of 1812 gained him a promotion to major. By 1829 he was a lieutenant colonel. With this rank, he led the army in a successful war against

the Sauk Indians in Wisconsin.

Old Rough and Ready continued to maintain his lifelong record of military victories without a single defeat. In Florida he crushed a force of Seminole Indians at Lake Okeechobee. He was elevated to the rank of brigadier general and placed in command of the Army's Department of the Southwest at Fort Smith, Arkansas.

Then, as trouble with Mexico reached the breaking point in 1846, it was Zachary Taylor who commanded four thousand troops sent to the Rio Grande. The Mexicans attacked, and Taylor soon had two more victories to his credit — the battles of Palo Alto and Resaca de la Palma. When

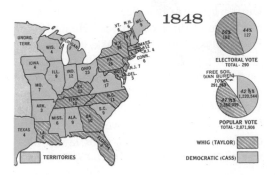

1848

ELECTORAL VOTE
TOTAL - 290

FREE SOIL
(VAN BUREN)
10%
291,263

POPULAR VOTE
TOTAL - 2,871,906

WHIG (TAYLOR)

DEMOCRATIC (CASS)

TERRITORIES

war was declared, Taylor led an invasion into Mexico, where he captured Monterey.

Politics now resulted in one of history's ironical twists. Fearing Taylor's rising popularity with the Whigs, Democrat James Polk assigned General Winfield Scott to lead the major invasion force into central Mexico, bypassing Taylor. But the move backfired when Taylor's force of five thousand men was attacked by twenty thousand Mexicans under Santa Anna at Buena Vista. Old Rough and Ready refused Ana's demand for surrender, fought it out and soundly defeated the Mexicans. This stunning victory rocketed Taylor into the very role of national hero which Polk had attempted to prevent.

The Mexican War terminated in 1848 with a treaty giving Texas and vast Southwest and West Coast territories to the United States. Mexico was paid fifteen million dollars under the treaty.

For a very brief time, Taylor went into retirement, but at their convention in Philadelphia, the Whigs nominated him for the presidency. His running mate was Millard Fillmore. As usual, the Whigs had no idea of their candidate's political ideas, but wanted a national hero to lead their ticket.

Taylor and Fillmore defeated Democrat Lewis Cass with 163 to 127 electoral votes.

Immediately upon his inauguration, Taylor shocked his Whig backers by making it clear he would be nobody's figurehead. He stood immovable in the face of bitter Southern threats of secession. Though he was a Southerner and a slave owner himself, he promised to lead the army, in person, against any rebellion. With California seeking admission as a free state, some of the bitterest debates ever to thunder in the Capitol began to rage. Meanwhile, Taylor saw the signing of the Clayton-Bulwer Treaty with Britain, guaranteeing neutrality of any canal built in Central America to link the Atlantic and Pacific oceans.

After sixteen months in office, Taylor attended ceremonies on July 4, 1850, for laying the cornerstone of the Washington Monument. Exposure to the hot sun made him ill, and he died in the White House July 9, at the age of sixty-five, with the slavery issue still at the boiling point.

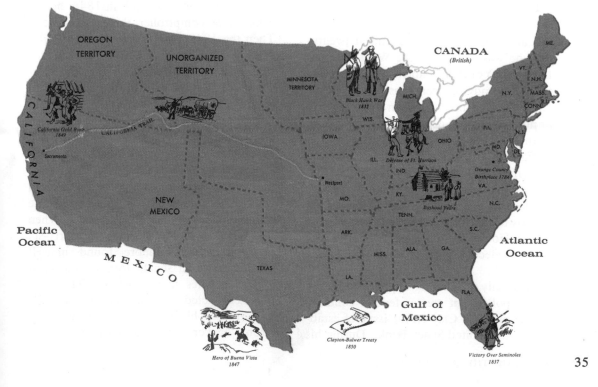

Millard Fillmore

The mid-nineteenth century might be termed a period of "log cabin presidents." Millard Fillmore, the second vice-president to inherit the highest office upon the death of a president, was born on a poor frontier farm near Locke, New York, located in Cayuga County. Young Millard grew up in a rough-hewn log cabin, toiled long hours with his father cutting timber and working the farm, often missing school in order to take care of crops and livestock.

At the age of fifteen, Fillmore was apprenticed to a local wool carder, who treated him badly for an unhappy period of four years. When a lawyer urged him to find another occupation, the eighteen-year-old Millard bought his release from the apprenticeship for thirty dollars, and with only four dollars to his name, he went to Buffalo. There he persuaded a friendly lawyer to assist him. By 1823 he had learned enough to be admitted to the bar. He started a successful practice in East Aurora, N.Y.

Fillmore had an easy, pleasant manner that won him friends. He soon found himself active in local politics, and at twenty-nine he was elected on the Whig ticket to the New York Assembly. While serving with that body, he won considerable popularity through his outspoken opposition to imprisonment for debts.

In 1830, he formed a law partnership in Buffalo with Nathan Hall and Solomon Haven. With increasing success in the legal profession came further demands for his services in politics. He was persuaded by friends to run for Congress and was elected to the House of Representatives in 1832. He was elected again in 1837 and served until 1843.

Generally, Fillmore supported Henry Clay's policies of greater federal controls, but he opposed Clay on the issue of establishing the United States Bank. During his

terms in the House he was helpful in putting through a grant of thirty-thousand dollars to Samuel Morse for the development of the telegraph.

Though he was defeated in a bid for the governorship of New York in 1844, he became state comptroller three years later. Then the 1848 Whig Convention in Philadelphia nominated Fillmore to run for vice-president with Zachary Taylor. Because of Taylor's dubious position in regard to the seething slavery issue and the fact that the Mexican War hero was a Southerner, the Whigs felt the need of a running mate to attract Northern votes. As it turned out, Taylor vigorously opposed the South's views on slavery and secession, whereas Fillmore took a more moderate stand on the whole slavery issue. When the Whigs won the election by thirty-six electoral votes, Fillmore found himself presiding over a senate torn by the most violent debates in its history. The vice-president acted with a calm impartiality that amazed his colleagues. He became a strong backer of compromise legislation.

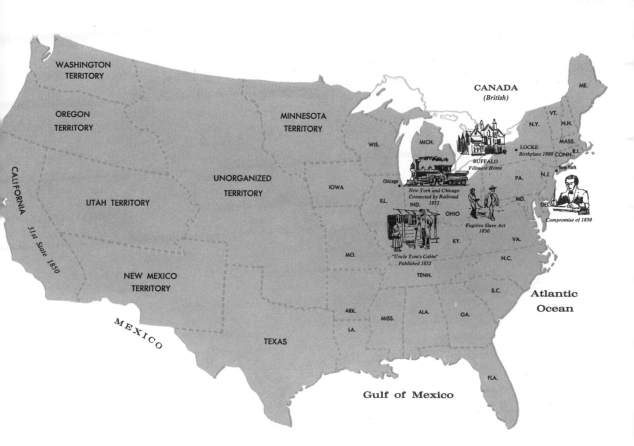

As a result, when Zachary Taylor died, July 9, 1850, and Millard Fillmore became president, the series of bills known as the Compromise of 1850 were quickly passed and signed by Fillmore. Through these instruments, slavery was abolished in the District of Columbia, California was admitted to the Union as a free state, Utah and New Mexico territories were organized with no specification as to their ultimate "slave" or "free" status. Included in the compromise bills was one tightening the laws concerning fugitive slaves for the protection of slave owners. Fillmore's signing of this particular bill cost him Northern votes and may have cost him reelection.

Fillmore had been eyeing Oriental trade possibilities and in 1852 he started Commodore Matthew Perry on a voyage to Japan, an expedition which was later to result in the opening of Japanese ports.

Meanwhile Fillmore's wife, Abigail, whom he had married in 1826, was in poor health, and their eighteen-year-old daughter Mary was assisting at White House functions. Mrs. Fillmore died shortly after her husband's unsuccessful bid for renomination at the 1852 Whig Convention.

Fillmore returned to law practice in Buffalo. He was nominated for president by the Know-Nothing and Whig parties in 1856, but lost the election. From that time, he lived quietly without much further political activity, although he was known to oppose many of Lincoln's Civil War policies. He died in Buffalo March 8, 1874.

Franklin Pierce

Handsome, well-to-do, cultured, and a brilliant orator, Franklin Pierce contrasted greatly with his predecessors in office. Pierce was the son of General Benjamin Pierce, a Revolutionary War officer who had served two terms as governor of New Hampshire. Franklin was born November 23, 1804, in Hillsboro, N.H., raised on a prosperous New Hampshire farm, and attended some of the best New England private schools, including Francestown, Hancock, and Phillips Exeter academies.

In 1820, Pierce enrolled at Bowdoin College in Maine. The debonair youth found himself at the bottom of his class after a year of gay parties and participation in literary and debating clubs, but he settled down sufficiently to graduate with honors, ranking third in the class of 1824. During his college life he became a close friend of Henry Wadsworth Longfellow and Nathaniel Hawthorne, classmates.

After graduation, Pierce studied law in Portsmouth, N.H., with Levi Woodbury, and attended Judge Howe's law school in Northampton, Mass. Admitted to the bar

in 1827, he opened a law office in Concord, N.H. It was not long before his personal charm and talent for public speaking led him into politics. He was elected to the New Hampshire legislature in 1829.

Next he won election to Congress on the Democratic ticket, serving in the House of Representatives for two terms. A staunch supporter of Andrew Jackson, he opposed the second charter for the Bank of the United States.

Pierce became the Senate's youngest member, only thirty-three, when he was elected to that body in 1837. Outranked and outclassed by elder senators, such as the great Henry Clay and Daniel Webster, he did little to distinguish himself. As his wife, the former Jane Means Appleton, was ailing and disliked living in Washington, Pierce ultimately resigned from the Senate and returned home to practice law.

With the outbreak of the Mexican War, Pierce volunteered as a private, but was quickly awarded a colonelcy in 1846. Under General Winfield Scott, he took part in the march on Mexico City. Promoted to brigadier general, Pierce commanded a brigade which attacked Churubusco. During this action he was injured in a fall from his horse. Though he courageously refused to let his leg injury keep him from participating in the next day's action, political opponents later accused him of cowardice because the pain of his injury caused him to faint during the ensuing battle.

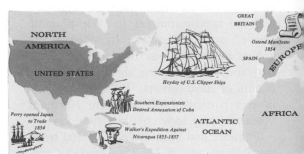

After the war, he made no effort to re-enter politics. But when the Democrats became deadlocked in the 1852 convention, Pierce's name was proposed by a Virginia delegation on the 35th ballot. Finally, Pierce was nominated on the 49th ballot in one of the most grueling conventions in the party's history.

Pierce took office under a cloud of tragedy. His last surviving son, eleven-year-old Benjamin had recently been killed in a train wreck, and he alluded to this briefly in the opening of his inaugural address.

His avowal that he would "not be controlled by any timid forebodings of evil from expansion" was borne out by his effort to annex Hawaii and the acquisition of additional Southwest territory from Mexico under the Gadsden Purchase of 1854. His policies also encouraged a group of American foreign ministers to seek annexation of Cuba. At a secret meeting in Ostend, Belgium, the ministers to England, Spain, and France issued the notorious Ostend Manifesto, hinting at the seizure of Cuba by force if Spain would not agree to selling the island. So unpopular was this move with most Americans that Pierce fell into disfavor even with his own party.

While the grieving Jane Pierce went into virtual seclusion in the White House, Pierce struggled to maintain an uneasy truce on the slavery issue. He foolishly signed the Kansas-Nebraska Act, a bill creating two new western territories in which the settlers were to be allowed to decide the slavery issue for themselves. The inevitable result was violence and bloodshed in the territories, as proslavery and antislavery forces battled for control.

Pierce was not renominated. Hoping to nurse his wife back to health, he took her on an extended European tour, but she died shortly after their return to the U.S. Pierce himself lived to criticize Lincoln's policies during the Civil War — a war which he felt could have been avoided. He died October 8, 1869, age sixty-five.

For all Pierce's support of proslavery elements in his party, he held preservation of the Union to be his chief concern. "Let it be impressed upon all hearts," he told his countrymen, "that, beautiful as our fabric is, no earthly power or wisdom could ever reunite its broken fragments."

1852

James Buchanan

served as a lowly private. Refreshingly, he was one of America's few public figures who was never even a commissioned officer, let alone a general with a string of victories to his credit.

After the war he threw himself whole-heartedly into politics partly to forget the tragedy of his fiancée's death. This un-happy affair affected him so deeply that he never married, but became the only bach-elor president to occupy the White House. His first success was election to the Penn-sylvania legislature in 1814. Next he went to the U.S. House of Representatives as a Federalist, but his admiration for Andrew Jackson led him to switch to the Demo-cratic party. In 1831, Buchanan was appointed minister to Russia, where he negotiated the first trade treaty between the two countries.

Chosen by the Pennsylvania legislature to fill a U.S. Senate vacancy, Buchanan served as a senator until 1845 when Polk made him secretary of state. It was Buchanan who administered the State De-partment during the Mexican War, and it was in this period that Texas, the South-west Territory and Oregon all came under U.S. jurisdiction. Buchanan's first bid for the presidency failed with Franklin Pierce's unexpected nomination at the 1852 con-vention, but Pierce appointed him minister to Great Britain, and in 1856, Buchanan won the Democratic nomination with little opposition. He entered the campaign in opposition to the first major Republican party ticket, which was headed by John C. Frémont. Former President Fillmore was also running on the Whig-Know-Nothing ticket.

Americans voted in a tense atmosphere brought on by antislavery slogans of the Republicans. On the other hand, Buchanan took a moderate approach to the slavery question, urging preservation of the Union

Like a volcano about to erupt, the na-tion seethed with sectional hatred when the fifteenth president moved to the White House. The man who was destined to be the leader when the first seven states seceded was scarcely to be blamed for the explosive situation leading to civil war. If anything, his broad political and diplomatic experi-ence might have contributed to solving any but the impossible problems he faced.

James Buchanan was another president of log cabin origin, as he was born in a humble cabin at Stony Batter, Franklin County, Pa., April 23, 1791. As a boy, he helped his father operate a country store, learning arithmetic through the practical experience of keeping the store's accounts. Meanwhile he studied Latin and Greek, which gave him a good classical foundation for his college education. Later he attended Dickinson College, graduating with top honors in 1809. He turned to a study of law in Lancaster, Pa., where he began to practice in 1812.

The outbreak of the War of 1812 im-pelled him to enlist in the Army, which he

as the most vital concern of the nation. The result was a victory for Buchanan, although he did not poll a majority of the total votes cast. He received 174 electoral votes, 1,838,169 popular votes. Frémont's count was 114 electoral, 1,341,264 popular; while Fillmore received 8 electoral and 874,534 popular.

Buchanan's first move to prevent dissension was to appoint a cabinet of mixed loyalties. He tried to fill various public posts with an equal sprinkling of Northern and Southern sympathizers. But the fire was already raging. Violence and bloodshed were daily occurrences in Kansas Territory. At Harper's Ferry in West Virginia, a radical abolitionist named John Brown tried to start a slave rebellion and was hanged as a traitor.

When Buchanan supported admission of Kansas as a slave state, the North was enraged. He faced a bitterly hostile Congress during the second half of his term. The Congress rejected Buchanan's attempts to enlarge the army and navy, to start construction of a Pacific railroad and of a canal in Central America.

He did not seek reelection, nor was he nominated. When Lincoln won the 1860 election, Buchanan saw the nation begin to split asunder. South Carolina seceded. Six other states — Mississippi, Florida, Alabama, Georgia, Louisiana, and Texas — followed in rapid order. The President dispatched *Star of the West* to relieve the garrison at Fort Sumter, S.C., but the ship was fired upon by Confederate troops. Despite this clear act of war, Buchanan ignored the incident since no bloodshed had resulted. Also, he was anxious to withdraw and to turn the agonizing problem over to President-elect Abraham Lincoln.

It is not hard to imagine Buchanan's sense of relief when he retired to Wheatland to write his memoirs. From retirement he urged Democrats to give full support to Lincoln in the prosecution of the war. He lived to see the war's conclusion, and died June 1, 1868, in Lancaster, Pa.

Abraham Lincoln

Mar. 4,
1861
–
Apr. 15,
1865

America has had her share of men who were great presidents. Some of these were also great men. Among the latter, Abraham Lincoln occupies a supreme place. Out of all the volumes written about Lincoln, it is difficult to form a true evaluation of the man. He was humble, shy, witty, dynamic, forceful, gentle, politically astute. He was understandably human and humanly puzzling. Occasionally, he said or did something that appeared outrageous or unwise, yet he emerged from every political or personal encounter with a quiet dignity and a greater stature than before. He transcended himself and his own weaknesses.

The rumble of civil war was growing to a roar as Lincoln's presidential campaign drew to a close in 1860. Southern states were threatening to secede from the Union if this self-educated country lawyer should be elected. Why? What sort of man was this rustic politician?

Abraham Lincoln was another "log cabin" president, born in Hardin County, Kentucky, February 12, 1809. His father, Thomas Lincoln, a wandering carpenter and farmhand, and his mother, Nancy Hanks, were both poor and of humble origin. Abraham spent much of his boyhood helping to clear heavily wooded land, building shelters and fences, hunting, and farming. He had scarcely a year of formal education. Books were rare in the frontier areas, and Lincoln was known to walk as far as twenty miles to borrow one.

In 1816, the Lincoln family moved to Indiana; they moved again in 1830, this time to Illinois. At that time, Abraham was twenty-one. He soon began to earn his living by plowing, husking corn, splitting fence rails, and chopping firewood; later he worked as a clerk in a country store. Often he would read until late at night. His books included the Bible, Shakespeare, and Weems' *Life of Washington*.

A tall, 6′ 4″, gangling youth, Lincoln was described as a "most uncouth looking young man." Yet his personal charm was very great. When he volunteered for service in the Black Hawk Indian war, his company elected him captain. Friends and neighbors persuaded him to try for the state legislature. He lost, but his own precinct gave him 277 out of 300 votes. He won the affectionate title of "Honest Abe" by repaying an eleven thousand dollar debt incurred in a partnership which failed.

In 1834, Lincoln won election to the Illinois general assembly. There his quick wit and readiness to debate attracted considerable attention.

Lincoln had been studying law with the help of John Stuart, a Springfield lawyer. In 1837, he began to practice in partnership with Stuart. Later he formed the law firm of Lincoln and Herndon, and achieved success representing business firms and corporations. During a brief term in the U.S. House of Representatives Lincoln had said little in opposition to slavery, but when passage of the Kansas-Nebraska Act

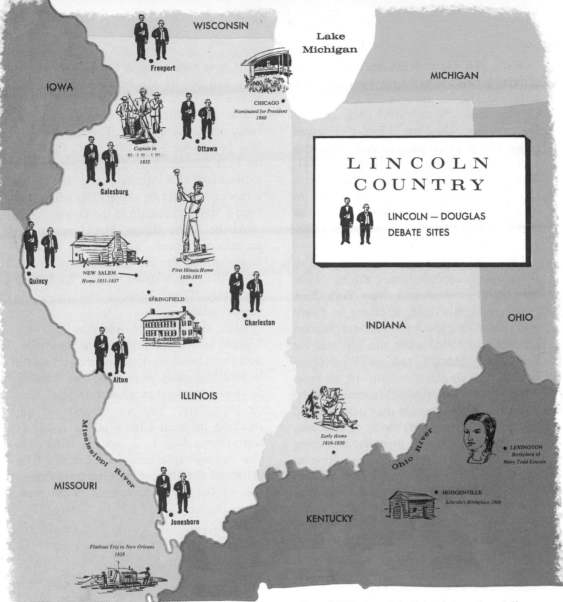

WISCONSIN

Lake
Michigan

MICHIGAN

IOWA

Freeport

CHICAGO
*Nominated for President
1860*

*Captain in
Bl k H wk W r
1832*

Ottawa

Galesburg

NEW SALEM
Home 1831-1837

*First Illinois Home
1830-1831*

Quincy

SPRINGFIELD

Charleston

INDIANA

OHIO

LINCOLN
COUNTRY

LINCOLN — DOUGLAS
DEBATE SITES

Alton

ILLINOIS

*Early Home
1816-1830*

• LEXINGTON
*Birthplace of
Mary Todd Lincoln*

• HODGENVILLE
Lincoln's Birthplace 1809

MISSOURI

Jonesboro

KENTUCKY

*Flatboat Trip to New Orleans
1828*

aroused the country, in 1854, he campaigned actively against the Act's supporters. In debates and speeches he made it clear that he was opposed to the principle of slavery. Then, as the Whig party began to break up, he joined the new antislavery Republican party.

It was in 1858 that the Republicans nominated Lincoln to run against Stephen A. Douglas for U.S. senator. In a series of famous debates, held in seven Illinois cities, Lincoln attacked Douglas' views on "popular sovereignty" and slavery so skillfully that newspaper reports of the debates placed "Honest Abe" in the national limelight. The South began to abuse, the North to praise him.

Although he failed narrowly in his bid for the Senate, he had become a prominent figure. His name was placed in nomination at the 1860 Republican convention in Chicago, and he won on the third ballot.

The railsplitter's bid for the presidency shook the angry South to its foundations. It was no secret anywhere that Lincoln had said, "A house divided against itself cannot stand. I believe this government cannot endure permanently half slave and half free."

With the Democrats split into two groups, Lincoln won the electoral vote. The tally was 180 for Lincoln, 72 for John C. Breckinridge, 39 for John Bell and 12 for Stephen Douglas. Lincoln received 1,866,452 popular votes as compared with a combined opposition vote of 2,813,741. Reaction was swift and drastic. South Carolina seceded December 20, 1860. In a short time the Confederate States of America had set up a government under Jefferson Davis.

On a fateful journey from Springfield to Washington, Lincoln toured through Indiana, Ohio, Pennsylvania, New York, New Jersey, and Maryland, speaking in towns and cities along the way. An assassination attempt was foiled when the trip was cut short and Lincoln entered Washington secretly for his inauguration. In his great address, he concluded, "We must not be enemies. Though passion may have strained it must not break our bonds of affection. The mystic chords of memory, stretching from every battlefield and patriot grave to every living heart and hearthstone all over this broad land, will yet swell the chorus of the Union, when again touched, as surely they will be, by the better angels of our nature."

But the "better angels" were momentarily overcome by hate. The terrible Civil War began April 12, 1861, with the firing on Fort Sumter, S.C. Lincoln proclaimed a blockade of Southern ports. By taking a moderate stand on slavery, he persuaded border states to remain in the Union.

At the White House, Mrs. Lincoln was an unhappy figure. Many of her relatives were fighting for the Confederacy and in 1862, their son William Wallace died. Only the lively "Tad" Lincoln brightened the somber mansion.

After the Battle of Antietam in 1862, Lincoln issued the preliminary Emancipation Proclamation, declaring that all slaves in rebelling states were to be free January 1, 1863. The final proclamation was issued on that date. The war thundered on, reaching its great climax at the Battle of Gettysburg, July 1, 2, and 3, 1863. On this Pennsylvania battlefield Lincoln later delivered the three-minute address that is one of the great documents of all time.

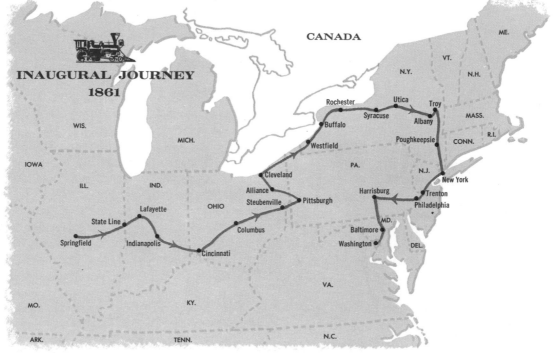

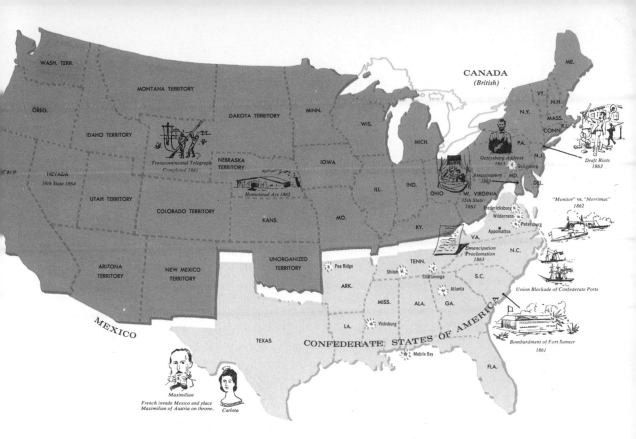

Many people instantly recognized its greatness, but in an age of flowery speechmaking, some critics found its simplicity merely silly. For example, the *Illinois State Register* commented, "Lincoln's buffoonery convinces the mind of no man," while the *Chicago Times* said, "Lincoln cannot speak five grammatical sentences in succession."

As the war still dragged on, it began to appear that Lincoln could not be reelected. But late summer victories in 1864 changed the public's attitude. He defeated Democrat George McClellan by a comfortable margin.

The surrender of Robert E. Lee took place at Appomattox Court House, Va., on April 9, 1865. Only five days later, at Ford's Theater in Washington, the Great Emancipator was shot in the back of the head by the actor John Wilkes Booth.

Next morning, April 15, 1865, Abraham Lincoln died. But Booth's bullet could not erase the words Lincoln had spoken a few weeks before: "With malice toward none, with charity for all, with firmness in the right as God gives us to see the right, let us strive to finish the work we are in . . .

to do all which may achieve and cherish a just and lasting peace among ourselves and with all nations."

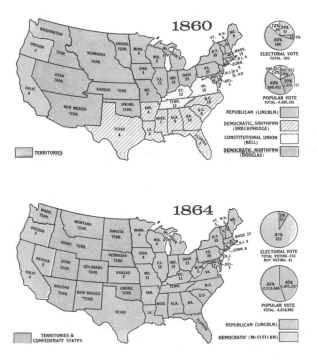

45

Andrew Johnson

Apr. 15,
1865
-
Mar. 3,
1869

Possibly no president, not even Lincoln himself, could have soothed the nation's temper or avoided the bitterness following the Civil War. Looking back it seems inevitable that any man who tried to steer a moderate course would have been attacked by those who wanted to heap vengeance upon the defeated South. Certainly Andrew Johnson, the only U.S. president who never went to school, was not the man to avoid a head-on clash with angry Northern leaders.

Johnson was a rough-hewn product of poverty. He was born in Raleigh, N.C., December 29, 1808, the son of Jacob Johnson, a constable, and Mary McDonough Johnson. At the age of ten he experienced the hard life of a tailor's apprentice, and at sixteen he ran away to strike out on his own. Like Abraham Lincoln, he had largely taught himself to read and write, studying whenever possible in his spare time. When he settled in Greeneville, Tenn., in 1826, he set himself up as a tailor and made a scanty living. A year after his arrival in Greeneville, he married Eliza McCardle, a

well educated girl who helped him to extend his own training. He took part in student debates in nearby colleges, thus gaining skill in public speaking.

As a result of his hard early life, Johnson became tough and stubborn in his support of the working people, but unlike Lincoln, who was of equally humble origin, Johnson lacked humor or patience. Often he angered friends and enemies alike by his attitude. Nevertheless, when he entered politics he won votes by his support of laws favoring poor farmers. He was elected alderman, then mayor of Greeneville. Tennessee farmers elected him to the state constitutional convention in 1834, and he served in the state legislature two terms.

After ten years of local politics he ran for Congress in 1843, was elected to the House of Representatives, where he served for another ten years. Finally, he left Washington to become governor of Tennessee in 1853. His fight for state support of schools was particularly popular, and he was elected to the U.S. Senate in 1857.

Johnson showed magnificent courage when he refused to go along with his state's secession. Branded a traitor by Tennessee leaders, he fled to Washington to escape arrest. He was the only Southern senator to take a stand for the Union and to refuse to join the Confederacy. As a result, when Union forces occupied Tennessee, Lincoln appointed Johnson military governor, an

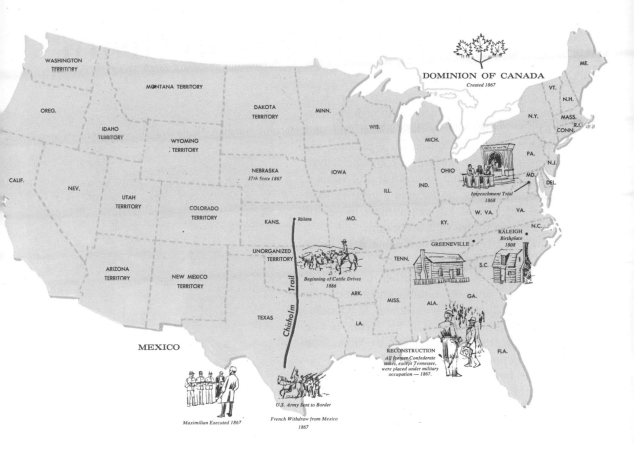

unpopular and difficult job which Johnson accepted in the hope that he could win back rebellious citizens by a generous policy. He succeeded surprisingly well. Tennessee sent representatives to Congress as early as 1864.

Elected vice-president in Lincoln's second election, Johnson represented Southern Union sympathizers. This was a Republican attempt to attract the votes of Democrats and of people in the border states. Six weeks after the inauguration, he was awakened late at night to be told that President Lincoln was dying from an assassin's bullet. Next day, Johnson was President of the United States.

Once again Andrew Johnson proved his courage by defying an unfriendly Congress, vetoing bill after bill which that body tried to pass in an attempt to punish the South. Johnson followed Lincoln's policy of am-

nesty. But Northern Republicans wished to keep all former Confederate leaders from public office. The fight became bitter. Congress passed the Tenure of Office Act forbidding the president to discharge an officer without the Senate's consent. Johnson violated this law by dismissing Secretary of War Stanton, who had worked against him Immediately the House voted for Johnson's impeachment, 128 to 47. But the Senate failed to achieve the two-thirds majority for impeachment.

At the end of his term, Johnson returned to Greeneville, Tennessee. After several unsuccessful attempts to get back his seat in the Senate, he won the election in 1875. He made only one rousing speech on the Senate floor, condemning his enemies. Then a sudden stroke of paralysis brought his career to an end. Johnson died at Carter's Station, Tennessee, on July 31, 1875.

Ulysses Simpson Grant

Ulysses Grant was a great man who never quite found himself, though the historical events of his time found him and thrust him into positions of greatness. He was a mediocre student, a complete failure as a businessman, an unsuccessful farmer. Despite all this, he became a great general and did a good job as president in one of the nation's most difficult periods.

He was born in a log cabin near Point Pleasant, Ohio, April 27, 1822. His parents, Jesse Grant, a leather tanner, and Hannah Simpson Grant, christened him Hiram Ulysses. They moved to Georgetown, Ohio, a year after his birth. It was in Georgetown that Ulysses, or "Lyss," as he was then called, attended school.

His father persuaded a local congressman to get the boy an appointment to West Point. By mistake, the congressman made the appointment in the name of Ulysses Simpson Grant. Young Grant never corrected the error. He had no desire for a military career, did not do well in his classes at West Point, but he showed marked ability in drawing and horsemanship. He graduated in 1843.

Grant was assigned to Jefferson Barracks in St. Louis as a second lieutenant. There he met and became engaged to Julia Dent. A few years later, at the conclusion of the Mexican War, they were married.

Like so many Civil War generals, Grant learned important military lessons in the war with Mexico. He fought at Resaca de la Palma, Monterrey, and Chapultepec, and was twice cited for gallantry.

After the war he moved with his new bride to Sackett's Harbor, N.Y. Then army orders sent him to Oregon. After two years of separation from his wife, he resigned his commission in order to return to the East. He tried farming and selling real estate, but was unsuccessful at both. Finally he went to Galena, Ill., to work in the leather shop owned by his brothers.

What might have become of Grant had there been no Civil War can only be guessed, but the outbreak of the war between the states prompted him to offer his services. The governor appointed him a colonel to help organize the state's regiments. In August, 1861, an Illinois congressman persuaded Lincoln to make Grant a brigadier general.

Suddenly the store clerk from Galena was winning victories. He led troops at Belmont, Mo., attacked and seized Fort Henry. When he demanded unconditional surrender of the Confederate forces at Fort Donelson, he became known as "Unconditional Surrender Grant" and was promoted to major general.

His great victory at Shiloh was an expensive one since it cost so many lives. The press complained of these heavy losses, Grant fell into disfavor and was transferred to command of troops in the West. But Grant continued to fight and win. In 1863 his victories at Vicksburg and Chattanooga gained him wide popular acclaim. Finally, Lincoln appointed him commander of all

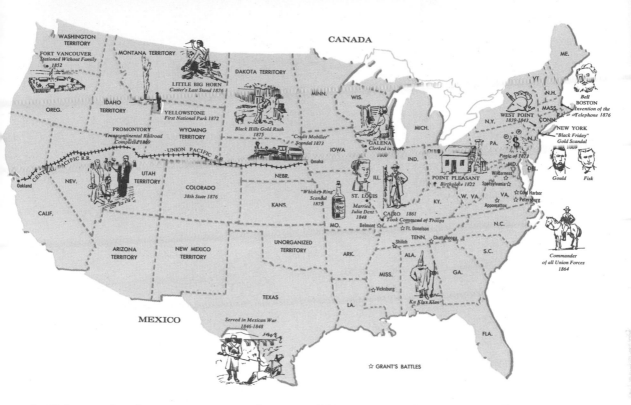

☆ GRANT'S BATTLES

the Union armies. As supreme commander, he accepted Lee's surrender at Appomattox Court House, Va., April 9, 1865. His generous gesture of allowing Lee's men to keep their horses "for the spring plowing" won him friends in both North and South.

Grant became critical of Andrew Johnson, and Republicans began to talk of nominating the popular general. He was nominated and elected in 1868.

As president, U.S. Grant was honest and sincere, but was frequently misled by corrupt advisors. Historians have blamed Grant for the corruption during his administration, but the fact is that the nation as a whole had been infected by corruption as a natural result of a long and terrible war. Actually, Grant tried to persuade Congress to pass civil service laws and to outlaw the spoils system, but the legislators refused.

Grant was reelected in 1872 by a greater majority than before. When financial panic and depression struck in 1873, he vetoed a currency inflation bill that could well have wrecked the nation's economy.

In retirement, after a two-year tour of Europe and the Far East, Grant invested

all his money in a banking firm. The firm's failure left him penniless in 1884. He then turned to writing his memoirs which, published by Mark Twain, earned one-half million dollars for Grant and his family. Two months after the book's publication, July 23, 1885, Grant died of cancer at Mount McGregor, New York. He died with the knowledge that his last work was an unqualified success.

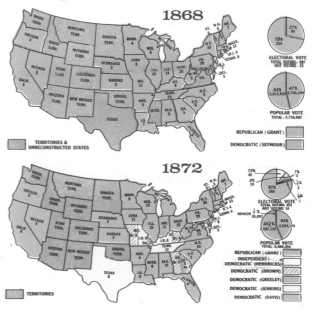

**Mar. 3,
1877
-
Mar. 3,
1881**

The man who followed Grant to the White House was one of the most honest of American politicians; a man of such high principle and moral character that when he won his first political election while fighting at the front in the Civil War, he refused to leave the field in order to campaign. In a period of national corruption, his brief term as president shone like a beacon in the dark.

Rutherford Birchard Hayes entered the world October 4, 1822, in Delaware, Ohio, the third son and fifth child of Rutherford and Sophia Birchard Hayes. He was always a bright student. An uncle Sardis Birchard, who helped tutor him, was hard put to furnish the boy with enough books to satisfy his studious mind. Young Rutherford attended secondary schools in Norwalk, Ohio, and Middletown, Conn., then went on to Kenyon College in Gambier, Ohio. He was valedictorian at his graduation in 1842. From there he went to Harvard Law School completing the course in 1845, and was admitted to the Ohio bar that year.

A law partnership which he formed with Ralph P. Buckland in Lower Sandusky (now Fremont), Ohio, was not very successful, and he later opened his own office in Cincinnati. During this period he attracted public attention by his sensational defense in two murder trials.

Rutherford married Lucy Ware Webb in 1852. Mrs. Hayes, a college graduate, did much to assist her husband's career. She was one of the most charming hostesses ever to grace the White House, and her moral objection to alcoholic beverages won her the nickname of "Lemonade Lucy."

Hayes volunteered for service with the Union forces when the Civil War broke out in 1861. He was appointed a major in the 23rd Ohio Infantry, fought in many of the early, violent battles of the war. After being wounded leading a charge at the

bloody battle of South Mountain, he was commissioned a colonel for gallantry under fire. Later, in 1863, he led the Kanawha Division in an attack on the Confederate John Morgan's raiders, trapped the rebels and captured Morgan. Hayes was breveted a major general for bravery in 1865.

He was still fighting when admiring friends nominated him to run for Congress on the Republican ticket. Despite his refusal to do any electioneering, he won the 1864 election. However, he did not take office until December 1865, after he had resigned his army commission. He was reelected in 1866. During his term in Congress, he worked to expand the Library of Congress and did much to improve the copyright laws.

In 1867 he was elected governor of Ohio. For three terms he made such an outstanding record of honesty, economy in government, and improved civil service legislation that his name was high on the list of presidential possibilities. To the worried Republicans, who feared a popular reaction to the scandals during Grant's ad-

ministration, Hayes was the perfect choice. He was nominated in the 1876 Cincinnati convention to run against Democrat Samuel J. Tilden. A close popular vote gave Tilden 4,300,590 to 4,036,298 for Hayes. The electoral vote was even closer. Also, there was some question as to the validity of electoral votes from Florida, Oregon, Louisiana, and South Carolina.

The dispute threatened to leave the nation without a president, but a special committee of five Supreme Court Justices, five Senators and five Representatives declared Hayes elected by one electoral vote. The decision came only three days before the scheduled inauguration. Hayes was already enroute to Washington before he learned of the result. After a private dinner at the White House on Saturday, March 3, 1877, with President and Mrs. Grant, he was sworn in by Chief Justice Waite so that the nation would not be without a president on Sunday, the legal expiration date of Grant's second term.

Hayes was tactful and politically wise. He somehow managed to avoid friction with Congress, although he pressed for civil service reform and for moderate treatment of the South. Under his leadership the last federal troops were withdrawn from Southern states, yet he showed no hesitation in the use of troops to stop riots in the railroad strike of 1877. His honesty angered the boss politicians. But Hayes had made it clear he did not wish a second term. Probably he would not have been nominated in any case.

He retired in 1881, devoting the rest of his life to work in education and religion. His death came January 17, 1893, in Fremont, Ohio.

51

James Abram Garfield

The era of the frontier log cabin was passing, and James Garfield was the last of the "log cabin" presidents. He was born in a humble log hut in Orange, Cuyahoga County, Ohio, November 19, 1831, the son of Abram and Eliza Ballou Garfield. Until he was sixteen, James went to a local school, meanwhile helping to work the family farm. But a restless nature drove him to leave the farm in 1847. He managed to reach Cleveland on foot, and to find employment as a deckhand and driver on an Ohio canal boat. In later years he recalled falling into the canal at least fourteen times and having as many "almost miraculous escapes from drowning."

A bout with malaria caused him to return home after about two years of rough life on the canal. By this time he was convinced that he must get a better education if he were to amount to anything. He worked his way through Geauga Seminary in Chester, Ohio, then entered Western Reserve Eclectic Institute (now Hiram College) in Hiram, Ohio. This was in 1851. In 1854, he enrolled at Williams

College in Williamstown, Mass. A brilliant student, Garfield graduated from Williams with high honors in 1856. He had no difficulty obtaining a position as instructor of classical languages at Hiram where, a year later, he was made president of the college. He was only twenty-six at the time.

In the meantime, Garfield was making a name for himself as a powerful speaker, preaching sermons as an unordained minister in the Disciples of Christ church. His vigorous attacks on slavery focused the political spotlight upon him at a time when the nation was approaching civil war over that explosive issue. With all this, Garfield found time to study law, was elected to the Ohio senate in 1859 and was admitted to the bar a year later.

Almost at the outbreak of war, Garfield volunteered and was commissioned a lieutenant colonel in the 42nd Regiment Ohio Volunteers. A brief campaign in Kentucky resulted in his winning a minor victory at Middle Creek, and a promotion to become the Union Army's youngest brigadier general. He went on to fight at Shiloh, became chief of staff for the Army of the Cumberland, and in 1863 was again promoted, this time to major general, for his gallantry at the Battle of Chickamauga.

Admiring friends helped to win him election to the U.S. House of Representatives. He resigned his Army commission in December, 1863, to take up his new duties in Congress. There, Garfield was so active in committees and in leading Republican fights for "sound money" policies and tariff laws, that he soon became the recognized leader of his party. He was reelected to Congress eight times.

Although he was unanimously elected to the U.S. Senate by the Ohio legislature in 1880, he never had an opportunity to take his seat in the upper house. A widely split Republican convention in Chicago, in 1880,

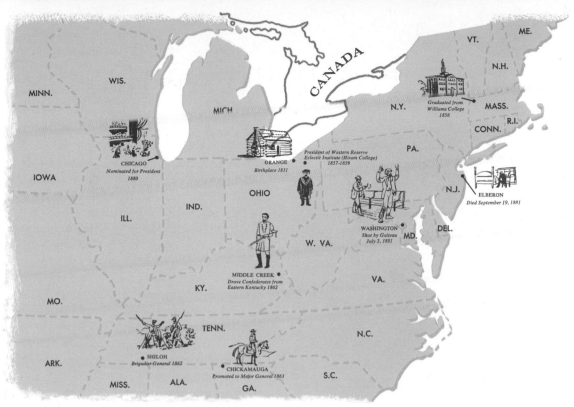

nominated James Garfield for president on the thirty-sixth ballot after reaching a stalemate between former President Grant and James G. Blaine.

It seems evident that Garfield did not particularly wish to be president. He showed a sense of impending tragedy when he told friends that he believed his happy life had come to an end with his election. The vote was a close one — 4,454,416 popular votes for Garfield, 4,444,952 for Democrat Hancock.

The Republican party split was deep and dangerous. Those who called themselves the "Stalwarts" were represented by Vice-President-elect Chester A. Arthur. Garfield, who favored the "Halfbreeds," found himself besieged by office seekers from both groups. Political corruption from Grant's days still infected Washington. Yet Garfield took office optimistically. On the ride up Pennsylvania Avenue to his inauguration, he was pleased to see a group of ex-Confederate soldiers waving the stars and stripes enthusiastically. In his address, he said, "Sacredly preserving whatever has been gained to liberty and good government during the century, our people are determined to leave behind them all those bitter controversies . . ."

But bitter controversies plagued Garfield throughout his brief administration. Much of his time was spent in trying to avoid disputes over political appointments. In a Washington railroad station on July 2, 1881, he was shot by a "Stalwart Republican" who had been turned down for the post of U.S. Consul in Paris. The assassin, Charles J. Guiteau, was arrested shortly and hanged in Washington a year later on June 30, 1882.

Garfield suffered through the hot summer, was removed to a seaside resort in Elberon, N. J., and died September 19, 1881. He was the fourth president to die in office.

1880

ELECTORAL VOTE
TOTAL 369

POPULAR VOTE
TOTAL - 9,218,951

TERRITORIES

REPUBLICAN (GARFIELD)

DEMOCRATIC (HANCOCK)

53

Chester Alan Arthur

There is something about the presidency that sometimes brings out the best in men. Until the day Chester A. Arthur became president of the United States, he was a machine, or "gang" politician who had made a career of the spoils system in government. Following the Civil War, corrupt practices produced more and more powerful political bosses who grew rich by selling favors and influence. One of these was Senator Roscoe Conkling, boss of the New York Republican organization. For several years, Arthur was Conkling's aide, and he used his position openly to advance himself and his party.

Chester Alan Arthur was born October 5, 1830, in Fairfield, Vermont, the son of a Baptist minister from the North of Ireland. Chester's family moved frequently during his boyhood. As a result, he attended a number of New England and upper New York schools. He graduated from Union College, Schenectady, N.Y., at the age of eighteen and became principal of the school in North Pownal, Vt., a short time afterward. He studied law, joined a New York City law firm in 1853, and was admitted to the bar a year later.

Arthur attracted public attention by defending Negroes. He won a celebrated case in 1855, establishing the right of Negroes to ride any New York streetcar.

After helping Edwin D. Morgan win re-election as governor of New York in 1860, Arthur was appointed to various state posts. It was thus that he became associated with Senator Conkling and the New York "Stalwart" Republicans. When President Grant appointed him collector of the Port of New York, Arthur used his authority to give out dozens of smaller jobs, in return for which the Republican party received heavy contributions from customs employees.

An attempt was made by President Hayes to clean up the corruption in New York. In 1877 he ordered an investigation of the New York Customs House. Arthur was suspended a year later. But at the 1880 Republican convention, powerful Conkling forces, failing to nominate Grant, succeeded in having Chester Arthur nominated for vice-president with Garfield.

The evil of machine politics and patronage reached a tragic climax when Garfield was assassinated by a political job seeker, and Arthur, the New York machine politican, became president September 20, 1881, at 1:30 A.M.

At this point the Stalwarts thought that they had a man in the White House who could be counted on to support their machine. They were disappointed. With the public now clamoring for civil service reform, Congress passed the Pendleton Civil Service Act setting up a system of competitive examinations for government jobs and making it unlawful to discharge civil service employees for political reasons. Arthur, who had supported the bill, promptly signed it and appointed Dorman B. Eaton, the Act's author, first chairman

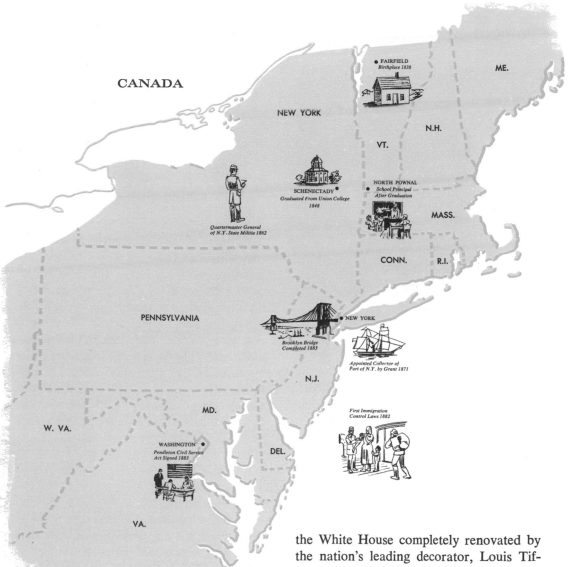

CANADA

NEW YORK

ME.

N.H.

VT.

MASS.

CONN.

R.I.

• FAIRFIELD
Birthplace 1830

*Quartermaster General
of N.Y. State Militia 1862*

SCHENECTADY •
*Graduated From Union College
1848*

NORTH POWNAL
• *School Principal
After Graduation*

PENNSYLVANIA

• NEW YORK

*Brooklyn Bridge
Completed 1883*

*Appointed Collector of
Port of N.Y. by Grant 1871*

N.J.

MD.

*First Immigration
Control Laws 1882*

W. VA.

WASHINGTON •
*Pendleton Civil Service
Act Signed 1883*

DEL.

VA.

of the Civil Service Commission.

Arthur next sought the prosecution of men involved in post office frauds. Though the accused men were acquitted after a dubious investigation, Congress passed laws designed to prevent similar situations in the future. When Arthur vetoed a bill authorizing huge expenditures to improve rivers and harbors, Congress overrode his veto. But the press and the public approved of Arthur's courageous stand.

During his administration, Arthur had the White House completely renovated by the nation's leading decorator, Louis Tiffany. This "extravagance" was one of the few acts Arthur's enemies could find to criticize. But Arthur, a tall man who enjoyed fashionable clothes and luxurious living, felt that the White House should be a showplace for visiting dignitaries. He and his sister, Mrs. Mary A. McElroy, entertained frequently and lavishly.

At the 1884 convention, Republican party leaders, angered by Arthur's reform policies, rejected him in favor of James G. Blaine. Arthur resumed his law practice in New York City for a brief time only, due to a bad heart. He died there of a cerebral hemorrhage on November 18, 1886.

Grover Cleveland

Mar. 4,
1885
-
Mar. 3,
1889

24th

Mar. 4,
1893
-
Mar. 3,
1897

By the 1880's, corruption in municipal, state, and federal government had become a major issue in elections. For years, Republican control of the presidency had been shaken by scandals, but until a Democrat of unquestionable honesty entered the presidential race, Republicans continued to win the elections.

The Democrat who succeeded was Grover Cleveland, called "Grover the Good" by admirers in both major parties. His record of honest and frugal government as mayor of Buffalo and then as governor of New York had attracted national attention, and he won the 1884 election after a particularly bitter, mudslinging campaign.

This stout, good-humored, and fearless fighter was the son of a Presbyterian minister. Stephen Grover Cleveland was born in a white clapboard house in Caldwell, N. J., March 18, 1837. The family moved to Fayetteville, N.Y., four years later. Grover received an average education in local schools, but after his father died in 1853, he decided to strike out on his own and travel to the West. An uncle persuaded

him to accept a clerkship in a Buffalo law office. There he began to study law and in 1859 he was admitted to the bar. By 1863, he had become assistant district attorney of Erie County, and he was elected sheriff in 1870. When he became mayor of Buffalo in 1881, the public began to hear about his sweeping reforms and his battles with dishonest politicians.

So riddled with corruption was the New York Republican organization at this time that when the 1884 convention nominated machine politician James Blaine, a group of Republicans known as the "Mugwumps" declared that they would support a Democrat for the presidency if they were convinced of his independence from machine rule. The Democrats seized a golden opportunity and nominated Grover Cleveland, who had recently opposed the Democratic Tammany Hall machine in New York City and had supported young Republican Theodore Roosevelt in his efforts to bring about city reform.

Cleveland won the election with 219 to 182 electoral votes.

As president he immediately sought further civil service reform. He made political appointments from both parties, saw that more jobs were placed under the protection of the Pendleton Act, and instructed members of his cabinet to rid their departments of extravagance and corruption.

Meanwhile labor strife was getting out of hand in many areas. A strike at the McCormick reaper plant was followed by a riot in Chicago's Haymarket Square, where a number of policemen and workers were killed. Cleveland urged Congress to establish a permanent labor arbitration board, but without success.

In 1886, Cleveland married twenty-one-year-old Frances Folsom in a wedding ceremony held in the Blue Room of the White House. She was the youngest first lady in

United States history.

Although he was renominated by the Democrats in 1888, Cleveland was defeated by Republican Benjamin Harrison. Yet Cleveland's popular vote of 5,540,309 was larger than Harrison's 5,439,853.

Cleveland returned to his law practice but continued to work as leader of his party. He was again nominated in 1892 and became the first and only president to win a second term after being out of office for a span of years. He took office for the second time facing a serious national financial crisis. United States gold reserves were dangerously low, the treasury was almost depleted, and the value of silver had dropped. Cleveland called upon Congress to repeal the Sherman Silver Purchase Act which had required the government to buy huge quantities of silver every month. He also had government bonds issued to replenish the gold supply. Panic and depression in 1893 brought about widespread unemployment. On top of this, Eugene V. Debs organized a strike of Railway Union workers against the Pullman Company. More violence broke out in Chicago, and in order to keep the U.S. mail moving,

President Cleveland sent federal troops to the city to end the strike.

At the end of his second term in 1897, Cleveland retired to Princeton, New Jersey, where he spent his time writing, lecturing, and serving as a trustee of Princeton University. He died at his Princeton home June 24, 1908.

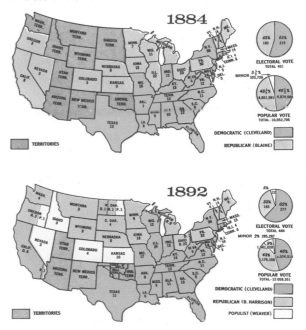

57

Benjamin Harrison

The Republicans' reputation of being "the party of big business" may have had its beginning in Benjamin Harrison's administration, for Harrison's vigorous support of a high protective tariff was approved by most business leaders of the time. Yet it was also under Harrison that the Sherman Antitrust Act became law.

The twenty-third president, a grandson of William Henry Harrison, was born on his grandfather's farm at North Bend, Ohio, August 20, 1833. His father John Scott Harrison had been a Congressman for the Whig party, and his great-grandfather, for whom he was named, was a signer of the Declaration of Independence. With such a background, his name had considerable appeal to the voters when he entered politics.

After attending a log cabin schoolhouse as a boy, Harrison spent two years at Farmers College near Cincinnati, then went to Miami (Ohio) University. He graduated from Miami in 1852. Though his boyhood ambition was to be a prosperous farmer, he became interested in law at an early age. His first job as a court crier earned him two and one-half dollars a day. From 1852-1854, he studied law in Cincinnati. He was admitted to the bar at the age of twenty-one, and moved to Indianapolis where he began to practice.

Benjamin Harrison's career began with great promise. He was an excellent speaker, a successful lawyer, and a respected lay member of the Presbyterian church. In 1857 he was a deacon, and by 1861 was elected an elder of the church. Meanwhile he had begun to mix in politics, acting as secretary of the Republican state central committee. In 1860, he was elected reporter of the Indiana Supreme Court.

In the Civil War, Harrison further distinguished himself. Commissioned a colonel by the governor, he commanded the

70th Regiment of Indiana Volunteers. He proved to be an able and courageous military leader, and was breveted brigadier general, January 23, 1865.

After the war, Harrison's success as a lawyer continued to bring his name before the public. But, in 1876, he failed in a bid for the governorship of Indiana. Despite this defeat, he was elected to the U.S. Senate and served from 1881-1887. As a senator he supported civil service reform, protective tariff, strengthening the navy, and veterans' pensions. All were issues which he later promoted during his presidency.

Democrats in the Indiana legislature managed to defeat Harrison's reelection to the Senate, but in 1888, when James G. Blaine refused to accept a second nomination, the Republican convention chose Harrison. The ensuing campaign was comparatively mild in comparison with the one which Cleveland won four years earlier. Harrison gave front-porch speeches at his home, while Cleveland did no campaigning, believing it was not proper for a president to campaign while in office.

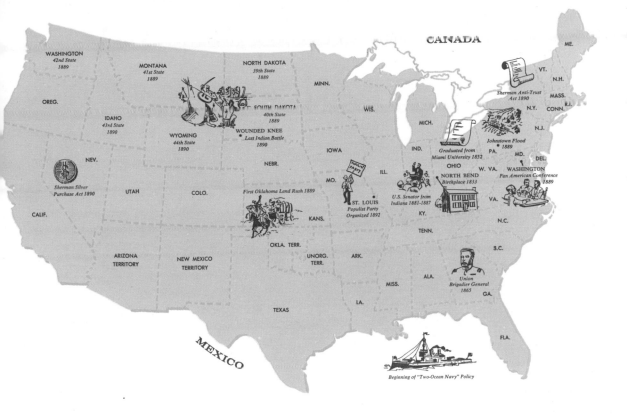

The outcome was an electoral college victory for Harrison, 233 to 168, although he trailed in the popular vote by nearly 100,000. He took office supported by a Republican Congress. This Congress quickly put through huge appropriations for federal projects, and the Democrats cried, "waste!" Harrison disapproved of some of his party's actions. But he seemed to have lost the courage he had shown as a military leader. He did, however, live up to a campaign pledge by seeing the Sherman Antitrust Act passed, and he started the creation of a "two-ocean" navy of steel ships. But his support of the Sherman Silver Purchase Act, requiring the government to purchase silver at an outrageous price contributed to the panic and depression of 1893, one of the worst in U.S. history.

His last important act as president, after he had lost his second election to Cleveland, was an attempt to annex Hawaii. But the Senate failed to act before Cleveland took office, and the annexation treaty was not ratified.

Harrison wrote a book about the government entitled *This Country of Ours*. In 1899, he went to Paris where he represented Venezuela in a dispute over the boundary between that country and British Guiana. Two years later, on March 13, 1901, he died at his home in Indianapolis.

William McKinley

The president who led the country in the gayest years of the "gay nineties" was himself a conservative with little gaiety. He was religious, devoted to his invalid wife, and rigid in his personal convictions.

William McKinley, the son of an iron founder, was born January 29, 1843, in Niles, Ohio. When he was nine, his family moved to Poland, Ohio, and enrolled him in Union Seminary, a private school. He attended Allegheny College in Meadville, Pa., prior to the Civil War, but discontinued his studies because of illness. For a time he taught school. With the outbreak of war he enlisted in the 23rd Regiment Ohio Volunteers. After engagements in the Shenandoah Valley and Antietam, he was commissioned a second lieutenant. He was promoted to first lieutenant, then to captain, and finally, in 1865, to brevet major. Later he served on the staff of Rutherford B. Hayes, whom he came to admire.

After the war, McKinley studied law at the Albany (N.Y.) Law School. He was admitted to the Ohio bar in 1867 and began to practice in Canton, Ohio. A powerful speaker, he soon became active in political campaigns. His speeches, in behalf of Rutherford B. Hayes for governor of Ohio, brought him before voters. In 1876 he was elected to Congress, serving until 1883. He served again from 1885 to 1890, and made a reputation as an outspoken champion of manufacturing interests. He fought for high tariffs to protect those interests. Soon he was recognized as Republican leader of the House, but his sponsorship of the McKinley Tariff Bill in 1890 proved unpopular and brought about a Republican defeat in the 1890 elections.

Meanwhile, McKinley's wife, Ida, had become an invalid, due largely to shock at the deaths of their two young children. Despite his busy life, McKinley devoted much time to her. He was often seen pausing on the street, removing his hat and bowing to his wife's hotel room window on his way to the Ohio state house.

In 1891 he was elected governor of Ohio and reelected in 1893. By now he was being discussed as a presidential candidate, and he had the support of wealthy industrialists and powerful business interests. The country was suffering a severe depression during Cleveland's second term. Gold reserves were alarmingly low. To oppose Democrat William J. Bryan and his "free silver" policy, the Republicans nominated William McKinley at the 1896 St. Louis convention. McKinley, supporting the gold standard

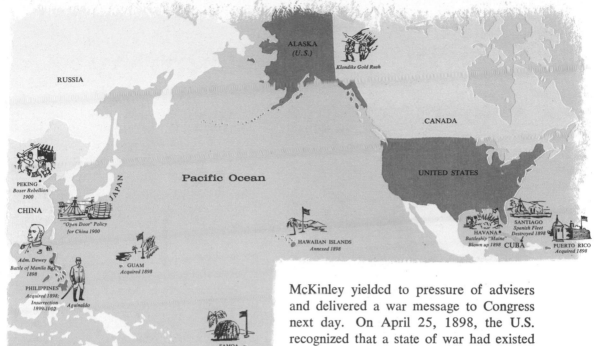

RUSSIA

ALASKA
(U.S.)
Klondike Gold Rush

CANADA

PEKING
Boxer Rebellion 1900

CHINA

JAPAN

Pacific Ocean

UNITED STATES

"Open Door" Policy
for China 1900

Adm. Dewey
Battle of Manila Bay, 1898

PHILIPPINES
*Acquired 1898;
Insurrection
1899-1902* *Aguinaldo*

GUAM
Acquired 1898

HAWAIIAN ISLANDS
Annexed 1898

HAVANA
*Battleship "Maine"
Blown up 1898* CUBA

SANTIAGO
*Spanish Fleet
Destroyed 1898*

PUERTO RICO
Acquired 1898

SAMOA
*Eastern Islands
Acquired 1900*

and "sound money," won a clear victory with 271 to 176 electoral votes and a popular majority of over 600,000. Yet he had limited his campaigning to front-porch speeches, refusing to leave his ailing wife on long tours, while Bryan charged about the country giving fiery speeches about silver and attacking trusts and the millionaire backers of McKinley.

As president, McKinley persuaded Congress to pass a high tariff act. Congress also passed the Gold Standard Act of 1900, establishing the value of the dollar as equal to 25.8 grains of gold nine-tenths fine.

Revolt in Cuba had been growing. When the U.S. battleship *Maine* blew up in Havana harbor, Americans clamored for a declaration of war against Spain. On March 9, 1898, McKinley sent Spain an ultimatum demanding peace in Cuba. By April 10, Spain had agreed to the U.S. demands. But

McKinley yielded to pressure of advisers and delivered a war message to Congress next day. On April 25, 1898, the U.S. recognized that a state of war had existed with Spain since April 21 when diplomatic relations between the two countries were broken. This war resulted in Spain's ceding Puerto Rico, Guam and the Philippines to the United States and abandoning her rule of Cuba.

Next, McKinley pressed for annexation of Hawaii, which Congress voted in 1898.

Renominated in 1900, McKinley rode a wave of prosperity into the White House for a second term, defeating Bryan by a larger margin than in 1896. America's new global outlook was stimulating trade and business, and McKinley called for an "Open Door" policy of trade with China.

Then at the Pan-American Exposition in Buffalo, September 6, 1901, President McKinley was shot by an anarchist named Leon Czolgosz. "Let no one hurt him," McKinley managed to whisper as he was being carried to an ambulance. He died in a Buffalo hospital September 14, 1901, the third president to be killed by an assassin.

Theodore Roosevelt

After the Civil War, the United States suffered a period of corruption in business and politics. Then public reaction put honest conservatives of both parties into the White House — Democrat Grover Cleveland and Republican William McKinley. But another change was stirring. It was destined to upset the nation's ruling interests, and the man who set off the explosive forces of social reform was catapulted into the presidency by an assassin's bullet.

The man was Theodore Roosevelt, a brash young politician who at forty-two had already electrified the country with his amazing personality and energy. "T.R." or "Teddy" as he became known to millions, was born of wealthy parents in New York City on October 27, 1858. A sickly child who suffered from asthma and nearsightedness, Teddy worked tirelessly to build up his physique. He graduated from Harvard in 1880, and married Alice Hathaway Lee the same year; but at her early death in 1884 he went to North Dakota to live the life of a rancher.

Roosevelt drove himself to feats of physical endurance. Told by doctors he had a weak heart, he proceeded to climb mountains, tend cattle for sixteen hours a day and assist in capturing Western bandits. In 1886 he returned to the East, then left for London to marry Edith Kermit Carow.

When his father died in 1878, he decided he needed to earn a living. "I had enough bread," he said. "What I had to do was to provide the butter and jam." He joined the Republican Club of New York at a time of its notorious corruption and quickly made a reputation for himself fighting for civil service reforms. At the age of twenty-four he was elected to the New York state assembly. Though he failed in an attempt to become mayor of New York, he was appointed to the Civil Service Commission by President Harrison and was reappointed by Cleveland. From 1895-1897, he was New York's police commissioner.

With some misgivings, McKinley appointed Roosevelt assistant secretary of the navy in 1897. It was not long before Roosevelt was stirring up the Navy Department, getting appropriations for building a stronger fleet over the opposition of Secretary of the Navy John D. Long. Teddy needled McKinley constantly about the Cuban situation, calling the president a coward for not taking action. When war was finally declared, T.R. resigned to command the famous Rough Riders cavalry regiment and as a colonel led them to victory up San Juan Hill.

This exploit helped him to gain the governorship of New York in 1898. In this office Roosevelt won popular acclaim and a host of political enemies by taxing corporations and by supporting reform legislation. The Republican machine, fearing his progressive ideas, tried to bury Roosevelt by naming him candidate for vice-president with McKinley at the 1900 convention.

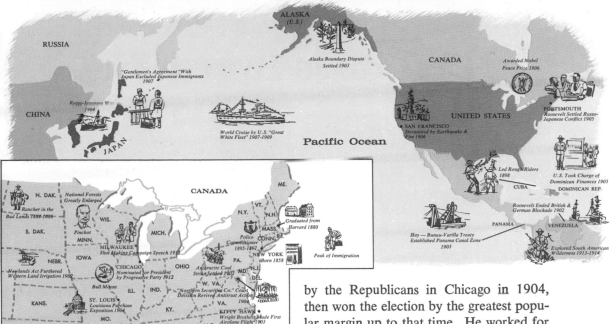

Once again, with McKinley's assassination, fate upset the political schemers. Theodore Roosevelt was sworn in as president on September 14, 1901, in Buffalo, N.Y. He soon plunged into the task of curtailing the power of huge corporations and trusts, thus earning the name of "trust-buster." At a speech in Philadelphia, he once said, "Unquestionably the great development of industrialism means there must be an increase in the supervision by the government."

Such sentiments alarmed powerful business interests, and the Republican Congress showed increasing opposition to T.R.'s policies. But he won wide public approval in his "Square Deal" program and his vigorous speeches urging honesty in business.

Meanwhile his dealings with foreign countries reflected the emergence of the U.S. as a powerful nation. He forced Germany to end a blockade of Venezuela, settled a Canada-Alaska boundary dispute, and speeded completion of the Panama Canal. For arbitrating a peace treaty between Russia and Japan, he won the Nobel Peace Prize.

Roosevelt was unanimously nominated by the Republicans in Chicago in 1904, then won the election by the greatest popular margin up to that time. He worked for conservation projects, adding 125 million acres to the national forests. A much-needed Food and Drug Act was passed in 1906, assuring inspection and sanitation precautions for the preparation of foods.

Refusing to run again in 1908, Teddy Roosevelt went big game hunting in Africa for a year. In 1912, at the urging of Progressive Republicans, he ran for president as the candidate of the Progressive Party. Though he was defeated by Woodrow Wilson, he polled more votes than the candidate of the regular Republicans, William H. Taft.

With the outbreak of World War I, Roosevelt offered his services to lead a division, but he was turned down by President Wilson.

This dynamic, tireless leader died of a heart attack at his home, in Oyster Bay, N.Y., on January 6, 1919. He left behind him one of the most exciting records in the annals of the American presidency.

1904

William Howard Taft

Teddy Roosevelt's handpicked successor to the White House turned out to be an unfortunate choice. The result was a split in the Republican party and a tragic break-up of the friendship between Taft and Roosevelt. Yet Taft's record as president was a good one by normal standards. The trouble was that Roosevelt's exciting administration made anything pale by comparison.

William Howard Taft was born in a handsome Cincinnati mansion September 15, 1857. He was the son of a prosperous lawyer, Alphonso Taft, who had served as attorney general and was a prominent Republican. William was large and heavily built. In later life he was six feet tall and weighed three hundred pounds. He was friendly, jovial, and a bright scholar. At Yale University he achieved excellent marks, graduating second in his class in 1878. He then went to the Cincinnati Law School, and after graduation was admitted to the Ohio bar in 1880.

Taft's lifelong interest was the law, and his greatest ambition was to become a Supreme Court justice. But his rise, like his bulky figure, was slow and ponderous. His first government post was assistant prosecuting attorney for Hamilton County, Ohio, in 1881. The following year, President Arthur appointed him collector of internal revenue for the first U.S. district. But when pressure was put upon him to discharge workers in order to appoint Republicans, he resigned and formed his own law partnership.

In 1887, Governor Joseph B. Foraker of Ohio appointed him to fill a vacancy on the Ohio Superior Court, and the following year he was elected to continue in this seat for a five-year term. As Taft's reputation grew, each succeeding president found a place for him. In 1890, President Harrison made him U.S. solicitor general, later he served as a judge of the Circuit Court of

Appeals. In this capacity, Taft handed down an important decision that labor has the right to organize, but not to make reprisals against industry that will be harmful to society.

When the U.S. acquired the Philippines from Spain, native guerilla war and unrest kept the islands in a turmoil. President McKinley needed a strong and wise administrator. He picked William Howard Taft, who served as civil governor of the Philippines from 1900 to 1904. Taft built roads, schools, post offices, and banks. He set up a judicial system and organized the government. His work in the Philippines was one of the great achievements of his career. Much as he desired to serve on the Supreme Court, he rejected two appointments by President Theodore Roosevelt to that body because he felt that his task in the Philippines was not finished.

President Roosevelt then appointed Taft secretary of war, giving him a host of duties and relying on him for advice in many difficult situations. So highly did T.R. regard his war secretary, that he assured Taft's

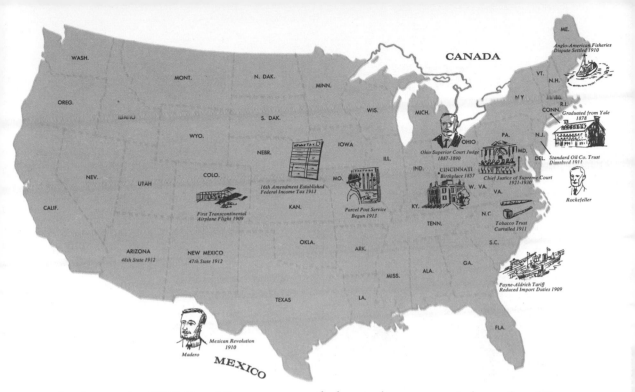

nomination at the 1908 Republican convention. The Republicans proceeded to defeat William Jennings Bryan for the third time, with more than a million plurality.

Taft took office, with serious doubts, during a wild March blizzard. He knew that the shadow of Teddy Roosevelt would haunt him. And though he tried to carry out Roosevelt's policies, he lacked the political shrewdness to handle the factions in Congress. When he attempted to put through a revised tariff act, he made enemies of both the liberal and conservative Republicans. The resulting Payne-Aldrich Act of 1909, reducing a few tariff rates, was highly unpopular with the voters.

During his administration, Taft started a federal budget system, established a tariff board to make recommendations on tariff legislation, sponsored a bill requiring political campaign expenses to be made public. Taft directed the prosecution of more trusts under the Sherman Act than had Roosevelt.

Nevertheless, the Republican split in 1912 cost Taft the election, although the combined vote for Taft and Theodore Roosevelt was greater than the vote for Woodrow Wilson.

Taft became a professor of constitutional law at Yale. Then at last, his lifelong dream was realized when President Harding appointed him Chief Justice of the Supreme Court in 1921. This was the job Taft had always wanted. He filled it well. Under his direction, the Court machinery was reorganized for better efficiency.

In 1930, Taft resigned because of failing health. He died in Washington, D.C., March 8, 1930, and was buried in Arlington National Cemetery.

65

Woodrow Wilson

Scholarly, idealistic Woodrow Wilson was a surprisingly tough politician and a leader who was not afraid to clash head on with tradition, or with the entrenched machine politicians. In his final battles, his idealism defeated him, but largely because his vision was far ahead of his time.

Wilson's background gave him an early appreciation of religion and learning. His father, Joseph Ruggles Wilson, was a Presbyterian minister who enjoyed reading the Bible and classic literature aloud to his family. Thomas Woodrow was born in Staunton, Virginia, December 28, 1856. He dropped the Thomas from his name during his college days. After the family moved to Augusta, Ga., young Wilson was largely tutored at home, for the Civil War had closed most schools in the deep South. He entered Davidson College in 1873, and after one year went to the College of New Jersey (now Princeton) in 1875.

Wilson was not an outstanding student, but his determination to advance himself took him to law school at the University of Virginia. In 1882 he opened a law office, which was unsuccessful. At this point he sought a career in teaching, went to Johns Hopkins University where he studied history and politics, and received the Ph.D. degree. He used his first published book on *Congressional Government* as his doctoral thesis. He taught history and political economy at Bryn Mawr College and Wesleyan University, then became a professor of jurisprudence and political economy at Princeton.

Elected president of Princeton University in 1902, Wilson tried to make changes in the organization of the University, and came into conflict with some of the trustees and some of the alumni. Though he failed to achieve his goals, his battles gained him wide national attention. New Jersey Democrats persuaded him to run for governor, and he was elected in 1910 by a large majority. Then he jolted his supporters by refusing to go along with the Democrat machine. He pushed reform bills through the state legislature, including new primary election laws, a corrupt practices act, and an employers' liability law.

At the 1912 Democrat convention in Baltimore, Wilson was nominated for president. He won the election easily against the split Republicans with 435 electoral votes to Roosevelt's 88 and Taft's 8.

Wilson continued to demonstrate his determined leadership by appearing personally to deliver a message to Congress, the first president to do so since John Adams. It was Wilson's view that the president should be the nation's moral and political leader; that he should propose new legislation to Congress. Now he urged the passage of reduced tariffs and soon had the satisfaction of signing the Underwood Tariff Act. Under Wilson's skilled guidance, the Federal Reserve System was established in 1913, while the Clayton Antitrust Act of 1914 increased federal

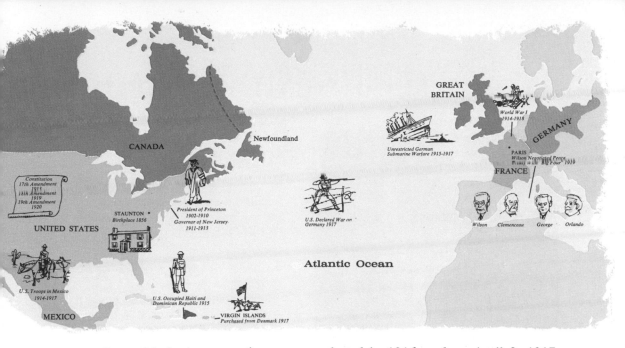

power to police unfair business practices.

Wilson was a devoted family man. He often relied upon the advice of his wife, the former Ellen Louise Axson, and he enjoyed playing games with his three daughters. When Mrs. Wilson died in 1914, he was deeply depressed, but he married again in 1915, this time to a Washington widow Mrs. Edith Bolling Galt.

Foreign affairs were troublesome and complex at this time. Wilson sent troops to Veracruz, Mexico, in a clash with dictator Huerta. He also ordered occupation of Nicaragua, Haiti, and the Dominican Republic at various times during 1914, 1915, and 1916. In these matters Wilson was firm, and he brought about the fall of Huerta's dictatorship in Mexico.

As World War I got under way, Wilson was less successful in his dealing with Germany. He sent a number of futile notes to the Kaiser while German submarines continued to sink American ships. Wilson was reelected in 1916, and on April 2, 1917, he appeared before Congress asking war because "the world must be made safe for democracy." Congress declared war on Germany April 6, 1917.

In a major speech to Congress in 1918, Wilson outlined his famous Fourteen Points for peace, the last of which proposed a league of nations. But he failed to achieve his great design when the experienced European diplomats made few concessions to the idealistic Wilson at the Paris Peace Conference in 1919. When the Senate rejected the League of Nations, Wilson went on tour to win support for his plan from the public. The strain proved too much for him. He collapsed after a speech at Pueblo, Colo., and returned to Washington where he suffered a paralytic stroke.

Woodrow Wilson received the Nobel Peace Prize in 1920, but he was a broken, disappointed man. He died February 3, 1924, in Washington, D.C.

Warren Gamaliel Harding

Mar. 4,
1921
-
Aug. 2,
1923

As the United States grew to a giant world power and passed the hundred million population mark, the presidency became a highly complex, backbreaking office. Certainly in the 1920's this was no job for a genial, handshaking fellow who enjoyed sports and easy living, and who had little knowledge of a president's vast responsibilities. It was a tragedy for the nation and for the man himself that Warren G. Harding should be pushed or enticed into the White House by ambitious political friends.

Warren G. Harding was born in Corsica, Ohio, November 2, 1865, the son of a physician Dr. George Tryon Harding and Phoebe Elizabeth Dickerson Harding. He was the eldest of eight children. After spending his boyhood on the family farm and attending a rural school, he went to Ohio Central College in 1879, where he remained until 1882.

When the Hardings moved to Marion, Ohio, young Warren went to work for the local *Democratic Mirror*. He was eighteen at the time. Shortly afterward he was dis-

charged for showing up with a Republican campaign hat. Then in 1884 he became an editor for the weekly Marion *Star*. Later he and a friend bought the *Star* for three hundred dollars and converted it to a daily. As the town grew, the newspaper prospered. Harding made some successful investments in real estate and lumber, becoming financially independent at an early age.

Meanwhile Harding had made a friend of Ohio Senator Joseph B. Foraker, who persuaded him to enter politics. In 1898, he was elected to the state senate. He was elected lieutenant-governor in 1904, but was defeated in a bid for the governorship in 1910. During this period, the 17th Amendment established popular election of U.S. senators. In 1914, Harding ran in the first popular senatorial election. He defeated his former friend Joseph Foraker in the Republican primaries, then won the election.

As a senator, Harding emerged as a man who could acquire friends easily, but who had little ability as a leader. He offered no new legislation and was absent from most sessions, spending a large part of his time seeking political appointments for his friends. Although he supported women's suffrage, he admitted that he had no interest in this or in other reforms of that period. His greatest interests seemed to be golf, poker, and enjoying social life.

Because he was handsome and "looked like a president," one of Harding's political cronies, Harry M. Daugherty, persuaded him to try for the presidency. At the 1920 Republican convention in Chicago, the smoke-filled-room brand of political maneuvering became widely publicized when the Republican bosses met to break a stalemate. They agreed upon Harding as a compromise candidate. Next day, Harding was nominated on the tenth ballot.

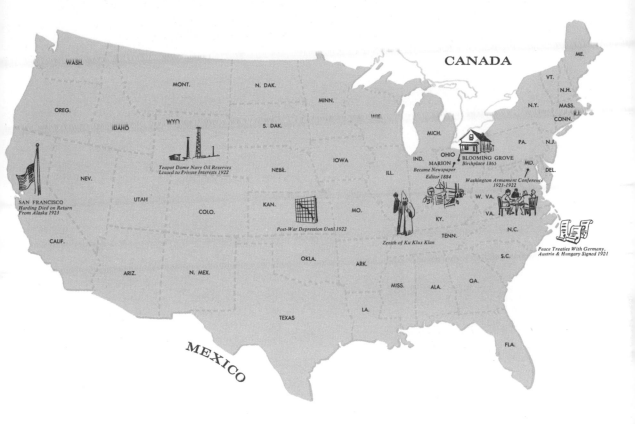

WASH.
OREG.
IDAHO
MONT.
N. DAK.
MINN.
WYO.
S. DAK.
IOWA
NEBR.
NEV.
UTAH
COLO.
KAN.
MO.
CALIF.
ARIZ.
N. MEX.
OKLA.
ARK.
TEXAS
MISS.
ALA.
LA.
GA.
FLA.
WIS.
MICH.
IND.
OHIO
MARION
ILL.
KY.
TENN.
W. VA.
VA.
N.C.
S.C.
PA.
N.Y.
N.J.
DEL.
MD.
VT.
N.H.
MASS.
CONN.
R.I.
ME.

CANADA

MEXICO

Teapot Dome Navy Oil Reserves
Leased to Private Interests 1922

SAN FRANCISCO
Harding Died on Return
From Alaska 1923

Post-War Depression Until 1922

Zenith of Ku Klux Klan

Became Newspaper
Editor 1884

BLOOMING GROVE
Birthplace 1865

Washington Armament Conference
1921-1922

Peace Treaties With Germany,
Austria & Hungary Signed 1921

A "front-porch" campaign in Marion, Ohio, resulted in a sweeping victory for Harding and Calvin Coolidge over James M. Cox and Assistant Secretary of the Navy Franklin D. Roosevelt. Harding's nomination and election had been too easy. He seemed entirely unaware of the pitfalls awaiting him when he confidently delivered his inaugural address over the first amplifying system to be used for this purpose.

Harding's campaign policy, "a return to normalcy" after Wilson's seizure of war powers, quickly found expression in his allowing Congress to resume leadership in proposing new laws. He killed United States participation in the League of Nations, once and for all, and continued to find government jobs for his friends. Dishonest politicians took advantage of the situation. By 1923, Washington was bursting with scandals, the worst of which involved Secretary of the Interior Albert B. Fall, who had accepted huge sums of money from private firms to lease government oil at Elk Hills, California, and at Teapot Dome, Wyoming. At the eleventh hour, the President became aware of these crimes.

Harding set out on a speaking tour in the summer of 1923, traveling to Canada and Alaska before he was suddenly taken ill. In San Francisco a few days later, on August 2, 1923, he died.

1920

ELECTORAL VOTE
TOTAL 531

POPULAR VOTE
TOTAL 26,759,723

REPUBLICAN (HARDING)

DEMOCRATIC (COX)

Calvin Coolidge

"Silent Cal" Coolidge inherited some of the worst political scandals ever to rock Washington when he became the thirtieth President of the United States. Coolidge offered a complete contrast to the hearty, genial Harding. He was closemouthed and shy, and he rarely smiled. Once when a guest at an official affair told him she had made a bet that she could get him to say more than two words, his only comment was, "You lose." At the laying of a cornerstone, Coolidge said nothing during the entire ceremony until it came time for him to turn a spadeful of earth. Then he picked up a small clod and remarked, "Good dirt."

Coolidge brought a frugality in speech and in the handling of money matters from his New England upbringing. He was born July 4, 1872, at Plymouth Notch, Vermont, the son of John Calvin Coolidge and Victoria Josephine Moor Coolidge. Calvin's boyhood was spent on a small farm, across from his father's country store. His early education was in the local stone schoolhouse. In 1891 he entered Amherst College, where he was graduated *cum laude*

four years later.

He read law with the firm of Hammond and Field in Northampton, Mass., and was admitted to the Massachusetts bar in 1897. Almost immediately he became active in the Republican party. He was elected to the Northampton City Council in 1899, served as city solicitor in Northampton from 1900-1901, and in the Massachusetts house of representatives from 1907-1908. He was mayor of Northampton in 1910-1911.

In 1905 he had married Grace Anna Goodhue, who was as gay and fun-loving as Calvin was silent and solemn. Despite his reserve, Coolidge continued to win political elections: to the Massachusetts senate in 1912, as lieutenant governor in 1916 and as governor in 1918. He achieved national fame in 1919 when he restored order in the Boston police strike by mobilizing the state guard. "There is no right to strike against the public safety," he told President Samuel Gompers of the American Federation of Labor, "by anybody, anywhere, any time." He was reelected in 1919 by a record vote.

The following year the Republicans nominated Coolidge to run for vice-president with Warren G. Harding. The ticket was victorious, and Coolidge became the first vice-president to attend Cabinet meetings.

While vacationing at his father's farm, Coolidge learned of Harding's sudden death. At 2:45 A.M., August 3, 1923, the presidential oath of office was administered to Coolidge by his own father, a notary public for the district. Coolidge entered the White House under the cloud of the Teapot Dome oil scandal and exposures of corruption throughout the Harding administration. While the public indulged in a spree of spending and speculation during the "Roaring Twenties," Silent Cal applied his

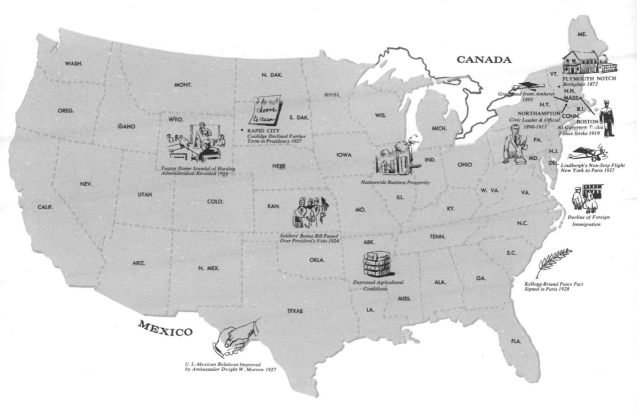

PLYMOUTH NOTCH
Birthplace 1872

*Graduated from Amherst
1895*

NORTHAMPTON
*Civic Leader & Official
1898-1911*

*As Governor Broke
Police Strike 1919*

BOSTON

*Lindbergh's Non-Stop Flight
New York to Paris 1927*

RAPID CITY
*Coolidge Declined Further
Term in Presidency 1927*

*I do not
choose
to run*

*Teapot Dome Scandal of Harding
Administration Revealed 1924*

Nationwide Business Prosperity

*Decline of Foreign
Immigration*

*Soldiers' Bonus Bill Passed
Over President's Veto 1924*

*Kellogg-Briand Peace Pact
Signed in Paris 1928*

*Depressed Agricultural
Conditions*

MEXICO

*U.S.-Mexican Relations Improved
by Ambassador Dwight W. Morrow 1927*

Yankee frugality to the government. He vetoed a soldiers' bonus bill, reduced the national debt by more than a billion dollars a year, backed an income tax reduction, and continued high tariffs for the protection of business.

In 1924 he was nominated for president by the Republicans on the first ballot, then won the election by almost a two-to-one popular majority over the Democrats. The Republican slogan was "Keep cool with Coolidge." In a booming economy some of the potential voters showed indifference to politics, and some showed confidence in the tight-lipped New Englander.

One of the most publicized events of the Coolidge administration was the Kellogg-Briand pact to outlaw war. That it failed to bring about permanent peace should not have surprised Coolidge who had said, "Peace will come when there is realization that only under a reign of law, based on righteousness and supported by religious conviction of the brotherhood of man, can there be any hope of a complete and satisfying life. Parchment will fail, the

sword will fail, it is only the spiritual nature of man that can be triumphant."

In 1927, Coolidge held a news conference at Rapid City, S. Dak., handing each newsman a note saying, "I do not choose to run for president in 1928." He did not even appear at the 1928 convention.

At the end of his term, he returned to Northampton, published an autobiography and wrote a series of newspaper articles on politics and economics. He became a director of the New York Life Insurance Company in 1929.

On January 5, 1933, Coolidge died of a heart attack in his Northampton home.

1924

ELECTORAL VOTE
TOTAL 531

POPULAR VOTE
TOTAL 29,090,208

REPUBLICAN (COOLIDGE)
DEMOCRATIC (DAVIS)
PROGRESSIVE (LA FOLLETTE)

Herbert Clark Hoover

No president of the United States was a better example of the American ideal of a self-made man than Herbert Hoover. None had greater personal success, both before and after his term as president. Yet his four years in the White House were filled with disappointment and frustration.

Herbert Clark Hoover, born in West Branch, Iowa, August 10, 1874, was orphaned at a very early age. He earned pocket money killing potato bugs and weeding vegetables; he helped put himself through college by delivering newspapers, managing a laundry agency, and doing a variety of odd jobs. When he was fourteen, he worked as an office boy for the Oregon Land Company in Salem, Ore. On this job he decided to become a land engineer.

In 1891 he enrolled at Stanford University, where he studied mechanical engineering. He spent summers doing geological work in Arkansas, Nevada, and California, graduated in 1895, and then went to work for a San Francisco mining engineer, Louis Janin. Through Janin, Hoover was given the management of some gold mines in

Australia. A brilliant engineer, he quickly made an excellent reputation. In 1898 he was appointed chief engineer for the Chinese Imperial Bureau of Mines. First he stopped in Monterey, California to marry Lou Henry. They spent their honeymoon sailing to Tientsin, China. When the Boxer Rebellion broke out in 1900, Hoover directed the building of defenses for the Tientsin foreign settlement. He next went to London, where he later set up his own engineering firm. By 1914 he was a millionaire, respected the world over.

At the outbreak of World War I, in 1914, Hoover was in London and was asked by President Wilson to set up a committee to aid thousands of stranded Americans. He then organized food relief for Belgium. In 1917 Wilson appointed him head of the U.S. Food Administration. After the war he returned to Europe to assist in rehabilitating war-torn countries. His work helped save millions of lives.

By this time, factions in both parties were seeking to nominate Hoover for president. In 1921 President Harding chose Hoover for his secretary of commerce and he continued to hold this office under President Coolidge. He was nominated for president on the first ballot at the 1928 Republican convention in Kansas City, Mo. The nation was enjoying the financial boom of the twenties. Prosperity was everywhere except in some farm areas and among the underpaid workers in the textile and mining industries. Hoover's campaign promise of

1928

ELECTORAL VOTE
TOTAL 531

POPULAR VOTE
TOTAL 36,744,939

REPUBLICAN (HOOVER)

DEMOCRATIC (SMITH)

"two chickens in every pot and a car in every garage" was doubted by few. He overwhelmed Democrat Alfred E. Smith with 444 electoral votes to Smith's 87.

Shortly after taking office, Hoover made a goodwill tour through Latin America. Then disaster struck the nation with the first of several stock market crashes occurring on October 24, 1929. As the Great Depression deepened, Hoover attempted to stem the tide with legislation. He called business and labor leaders to Washington, asked Congress to pass the Reconstruction Finance Corporation bill to aid banks and businesses and to lend some 300 million dollars for relief of the unemployed. Laws were passed to extend credit to homeowners, and public works were greatly increased. But the depression was worldwide. It had been brought on by unwise speculation, waste, corruption, and bad business practices of millions of people.

Meanwhile, this administration started construction of Boulder (now Hoover) Dam, added millions of acres to national parks and forests, established the Federal Power and Federal Radio Commissions. Hoover ordered the Marines to leave Nicaragua and reached an agreement with Haiti for the removal of U.S. troops by 1934.

Though he was renominated in 1932, Hoover and his party had little hope of victory. When Franklin Roosevelt won by a landslide, Hoover returned to his Palo Alto home where he wrote, lectured, and served as a trustee of Stanford University. He served on a committee to collect relief funds for Finland after the Russo-Finnish war of 1940. President Truman appointed him chairman of the Famine Emergency Commission after World War II, and to the famous Hoover Commission to study reorganization of the executive branch of the government.

Hoover continued to write books, lecture and act as the revered elder statesman of the Republican party until his death in New York City on October 20, 1964.

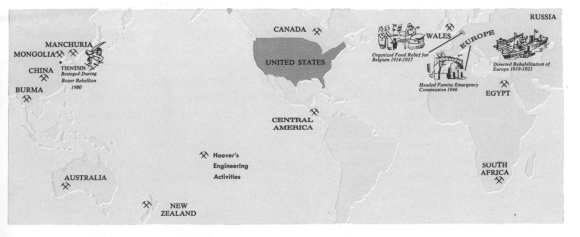

32nd Franklin Delano Roosevelt

Mar. 4, 1933
-
Apr. 12, 1945

The president who guided the United States government through most of World War II did not live to see the final victory. He was the man who, more than any other, brought into being a whole new philosophy of government in America. He called it the "New Deal." Franklin Roosevelt was idolized by millions who, in the depth of hard times, were thrilled by his stirring oratory and by his actions.

The Roosevelt New Deal started as an emergency approach to the country's worst depression, but the resulting social legislation changed the United States greatly from the pre-depression days. For better or worse, the U.S. has developed a kind of mixed economy, and the Democratic party has largely followed Roosevelt's ideas ever since. Generally speaking, the New Deal ideas of government welfare are supported by the "liberals." While there are "liberals" in the Republican party, more Republicans would be classed as "conservatives," who favor decentralization of political power and a balanced budget. In many ways, the terms "liberal" and "conservative" in the 1960's are the opposites of their political meaning in Jefferson's day. Jefferson, considered a liberal, favored limited government. Hamilton, a conservative, wanted stronger government controls.

The man who led America's great social movement, Franklin Delano Roosevelt, was born in a Hyde Park, N.Y., mansion January 30, 1882. His wealthy parents gave him special tutoring, yearly trips to Europe, then sent him to Groton School, in Groton, Mass., in 1896. From there he went to Harvard University. He became editor of the Harvard *Crimson* and took part in rowing and football. After graduation in 1904, he enrolled at Columbia Law School. Although he passed the bar examination in 1907, he left school before earning a degree, and he showed little enthusiasm for

the legal profession.

Meanwhile, against his domineering mother's wishes, he became engaged to his distant cousin Anna Eleanor Roosevelt, whom he married in 1905. The bride was given in marriage by her uncle Theodore Roosevelt, who was President of the United States at that time.

F.D.R., as he was known, began his political career by winning a New York state senate seat in 1910, the first Democrat elected from his district in over fifty years. He then proceeded to anger the Tammany Hall bosses by leading a fight against a U.S. Senate candidate, who had been selected by that political machine.

Roosevelt actively supported Woodrow Wilson in 1912, and a year later President Wilson appointed him assistant secretary of the Navy, though he had little experience to qualify him for the post. When Roosevelt ran for the U.S. Senate in 1914, he was defeated. But in his Navy Department post, he did a good job, working tirelessly on antisubmarine plans during World War I. He earned a reputation as a man who

got things done.

Roosevelt was only thirty-eight when he was nominated by the Democrat party for vice-president with James M. Cox in 1920. However, the Harding-Coolidge victory temporarily interrupted his political career, and he became a vice-president in charge of the New York office of the Fidelity and Deposit Company of Maryland. The next year, in August 1921, on vacation at Campobello Island, Canada, he fell into icy water while sailing, and was chilled. Within three days he had developed a severe case of polio. He lost the use of his legs and had partial paralysis of his arms and hands. With amazing courage, he fought back, regained the use of his arms and learned to walk with braces. Many of his friends were sure that his political career was at an end, but Roosevelt was determined to make a comeback. He spent considerable time at Warm Springs, Ga., trying to effect a cure. In 1926 he bought the springs and a huge tract of land surrounding them. Soon afterward he established the Georgia Warm Springs Foundation to assist polio victims.

By 1928, F.D.R. was back in politics. He supported the nomination of Alfred E. Smith for president, then won the governorship of New York by a narrow margin. Here was his first opportunity to put his liberal ideas into operation. He gained tax relief for farmers and as the depression deepened in 1930, proposed far-reaching relief for the state's unemployed. He also created a power authority to develop waterpower from the St. Lawrence River, initiated old-age pensions, conservation and reforestation bills. His popular program won him reelection in 1930.

Now Roosevelt eyed the presidency, and he persuaded James A. Farley, the Democrats' party chairman, to direct his campaign. At the 1932 Democratic convention in Chicago, Roosevelt won the nomination on the fourth ballot. In an acceptance speech he promised the country a "new deal" and an end to the depression. He promised a balanced budget, relief for the unemployed, and an end of liquor prohibition. A landslide victory gave him 472 electoral votes to Hoover's 59, and the United States was launched on the greatest social revolution in its history. In his ringing voice, F.D.R. had electrified Americans by telling them that their generation had "a rendezvous with Destiny."

So many banks were failing when Roosevelt took office, that he considered drastic action necessary. Two days after his inauguration he declared a "bank holiday." All the nation's banks closed. The Treasury Department proceeded to examine their books. Sound banks were allowed to open. Others stayed closed until they could be reorganized. Many never reopened.

75

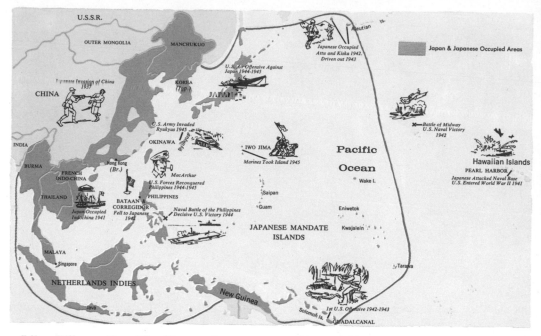

Like Wilson, Franklin Roosevelt proposed new legislation to Congress. He called for a series of emergency bills, most of which were passed during the "Hundred Days" of a special Congressional session in 1933. These included the Agricultural Adjustment Act, the Tennessee Valley Authority Act, and the National Industrial Recovery Act.

Meanwhile, Roosevelt explained his ideas to the public via radio. His famous "fireside chats" became an American institution in the 1930's.

Roosevelt's advisers, called the "Brain Trust," continued to suggest projects to end the economic depression. A Civilian Conservation Corps put one-half million young men to work on reforestation and other similar programs. The WPA, or Works Progress Administration, provided "made-work" for about two million people from

1935 to 1941. Yet the Great Depression continued. Far from balancing the budget, Roosevelt increased the national debt by leaps and bounds.

In 1933, the twenty-first Amendment ended Prohibition. The Social Security Act was passed in 1935, and in the same year the National Labor Relations Act gave labor the machinery for collective bargaining with industry. Roosevelt's "Good Neighbor" policy with South American countries greatly improved U.S. relations to the south. F.D.R. became the first president to visit South America when he went to Colombia in 1934.

Reelected in 1936, Roosevelt was angered by the Supreme Court's rulings that a number of New Deal acts were unconstitutional. He endeavored to reorganize the Court and was accused of trying to "pack" it with handpicked justices.

As World War II exploded with Germany's invasion of Poland, September 1, 1939, Roosevelt pursued a policy of helping Britain and France by all means short of war. Nominated for an unprecedented third term in 1940, he reassured isolationist America by saying he "hated war" and by promising mothers of America that their sons "would never be sent to fight in foreign wars." But after Japan attacked Pearl Harbor on December 7, 1941, the U.S. was plunged into the greatest war in history. Roosevelt had already met with Winston Churchill on a cruiser off the coast of Newfoundland in 1940, and had helped draft the Atlantic Charter, stating that neither U.S. nor Britain sought any new territory. After the U.S. entered the war, Roosevelt held several "Big Three" conferences with Churchill and Joseph Stalin: one at Casablanca, Morocco, in 1943, one at Tehran, Iran, in 1943, and his last at Yalta in the Crimea, 1945.

Elected to his fourth term in 1944, Roosevelt's health was failing noticeably. In March, 1945, he went to Warm Springs in an effort to regain his strength. On April 12, 1945, while working at his desk, he collapsed, complaining of a terrible headache. A few hours later, F.D.R. was dead.

Perhaps the world remembers Roosevelt best for his "Four Freedoms," which he outlined in a famous speech delivered in 1941. There is no question that his fight to insure freedom of speech, freedom of worship, freedom from want, and freedom from fear inspired all the world during some of history's darkest years.

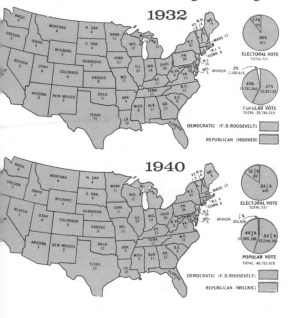

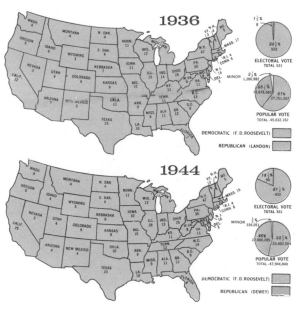

Harry S. Truman

Upon the death of Franklin D. Roosevelt, April 12, 1945, Harry Truman became the seventh vice-president to inherit the presidency. In many respects he had the most difficult task ever to fall upon a vice-president's shoulders. Fortunately for the United States, Truman was tough, aggressive, and courageous, and he proved himself to be equal to some of the most momentous decisions in history.

Truman was born in Lamar, Mo., on May 8, 1884. He was the oldest of the three children of John Anderson Truman and Martha Ellen Young Truman. When the family moved to Independence, Mo., in 1890, Harry attended the Independence schools. As he was forced to wear glasses, he seldom took part in rough games. Instead he devoted hours of spare time to reading, thus gaining a wide knowledge of American history, one of his favorite subjects. As a youth, he held a variety of jobs — with the Santa Fe Railroad, the *Kansas City Star,* and as a clerk and bookkeeper in Kansas City banks.

In World War I he distinguished himself

as an artillery officer, winning promotion to captain, then major. He saw action at St. Mihiel, Sommedieu, and Meuse-Argonne.

After the war, in 1919, Truman married Elizabeth Virginia Wallace, his childhood sweetheart. He then invested in a men's clothing store in Kansas City, but the business failed during a depression in 1921.

With the help of Tom Pendergast, boss of the Kansas City Democrat machine, he entered politics and was elected a judge of Jackson County, in 1922. Later, as a presiding county judge, 1926-1934, he gained a reputation for honest efficiency. Yet he was surrounded by a corrupt party machine, and when he was elected to the U.S. Senate in 1934, he led an investigation that uncovered many voting and financial frauds involving his Missouri friends, including Tom Pendergast.

Truman then won reelection to the Senate in 1940 without the help of the Pendergast machine.

As World War II developed, 1941-1944, Truman became chairman of a Senatorial Committee to Investigate the National Defense Program. He helped to save the taxpayers millions of dollars by cutting down waste and corruption in the handling of defense contracts.

In 1944, at the Philadelphia Democratic Convention, Truman was selected to be F.D.R.'s running mate. Roosevelt won an easy fourth term victory, but eighty-three days after the inauguration, Vice-President

1948

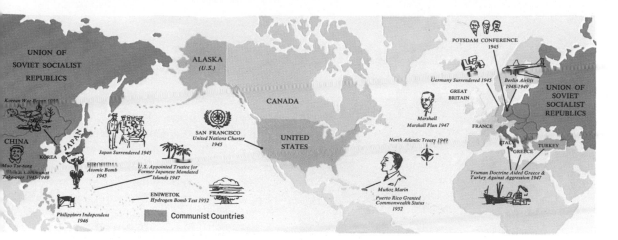

Truman was called to the White House to be sworn in as president. Next day, he told a group of reporters. "Boys, when they told me yesterday what had happened, I felt like the moon and stars and all the planets had fallen on me . . . If you fellows ever pray, pray for me now."

The war with Germany was nearing an end when Truman took office. Germany surrendered on May 8, 1945, and Truman held a conference with Churchill and Stalin at Potsdam, Germany, in July, 1945. While in Germany, Truman learned that the atom bomb had been perfected. He was faced with one of the most terrifying decisions in the world's history. Characteristically, it did not take him long to make up his mind. He ordered U.S. planes to drop the bomb on Japan, and the first one struck Hiroshima August 6, 1945. The second fell on Nagasaki August 9. As a result, Japan surrendered on August 14.

Vigorous, quick-tempered and outspoken, Truman was winning public respect. He liked brisk, early morning walks, enjoyed playing the piano, had a sharp tongue, and his salty comments made headlines. Russian expansion in Europe and Asia was opposed in 1947 by a tough "Truman Doctrine," guaranteeing U.S. aid to nations resisting communism. He approved the Marshall Plan, proposed by Secretary of State George C. Marshall, providing money grants to war-torn countries in Europe.

All the political experts predicted Tru-

man's defeat in 1948, but even with his party split between the Progressive Party and the Dixiecrats, he made a personal 31,000-mile campaign tour and upset all the pre-election polls with 303 electoral votes to 189 for Thomas E. Dewey.

In 1950, Truman made another fateful decision when Communist forces invaded South Korea. Without waiting for the United Nations to act, he sent U.S. troops and planes to the defense of South Korea.

Toward the end of his second term, infiltration of some communists into government was revealed, and Julius and Ethel Rosenberg were convicted of selling atom bomb secrets to Russia. These events contributed to Republican gains in the 1950 and 1952 Congressional elections.

Truman decided not to run again in 1952. He retired to his home in Independence, Mo., where he wrote his memoirs and continued to be an active party leader.

Dwight David Eisenhower

Until he became president, Dwight Eisenhower's career was that of a professional soldier. He was born in Denison, Texas, October 14, 1890, received his early schooling in Abilene, Kansas, then entered West Point Military Academy shortly after his graduation from high school. Eisenhower graduated from West Point in 1915, 61st in a class of 164. When he was assigned to Fort Sam Houston near San Antonio, Texas, he met and married Mamie Geneva Doud.

Eisenhower soon demonstrated his great executive ability. He became commander of a tank training center near Gettysburg in 1918, and served as executive officer of Camp Gaillard in the Panama Canal Zone from 1922 to 1924. He then attended the Command and General Staff School in Fort Leavenworth, Kansas, mastering a course so difficult that many officers cracked under the strain. Eisenhower graduated first of 275 men in the class of 1926. He was appointed General Douglas MacArthur's aide and went with MacArthur to the Philippines in 1935. There he organized a

Philippine Military Academy and learned to fly an airplane. He was the first U.S. president to hold a pilot's license.

By March, 1941, Eisenhower was a full colonel. Later that year, as chief of staff of the Third Army he was promoted to brigadier general, and was appointed to the War Plans Division in December. He helped to develop World War II master strategy for Pacific defense and for the Allied invasion of Europe, becoming commanding general of American forces in Europe, commander of the North African invasion and supreme commander of the Allied invasion of Normandy.

After the war, in 1948, he served briefly as president of Columbia University and wrote the best-selling book *Crusade in Europe*. By the time he was appointed supreme commander of NATO in 1950, both parties were asking him to run for the presidency. At first he refused, but finally resigned from the Army in 1952 to work for the Republican nomination. He won the nomination on the first ballot at the

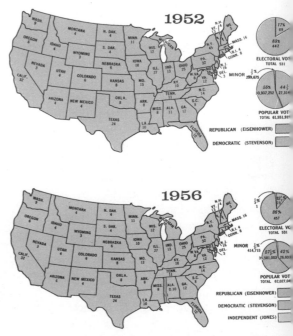

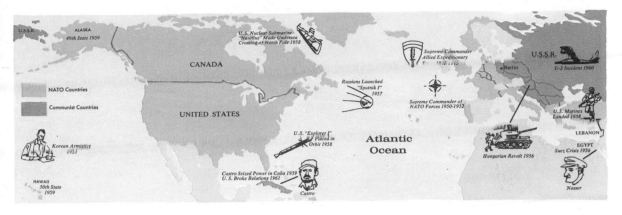

1952 Chicago convention. Calling his mission to the presidency a crusade, he won a landslide victory with 442 electoral votes to Adlai E. Stevenson's 89.

A deeply religious man, Eisenhower led off his inaugural address with a "little private prayer," heard by the entire nation on radio and television. He fulfilled a campaign promise by flying to the Korean battlefront to see the situation firsthand. He was unable to end the war at once, yet it was terminated by the summer of 1953.

Under Eisenhower's administration social security benefits were extended, the minimum wage was increased, a Department of Health, Education, and Welfare was created. Canada and the U.S. undertook the building of the St. Lawrence Seaway, which was completed in 1959.

In December, 1953, Eisenhower delivered a dramatic address to the United Nations Assembly, calling for the nations to pool their scientific knowledge to use atomic power for peaceful purposes. The "Atoms for Peace" plan was endorsed by sixty-two nations which organized the International Atomic Energy Agency.

Eisenhower, with Secretary of State John Foster Dulles, in 1954, formed the Southeast Asia Treaty Organization to resist communism. He proposed that Russia and the U.S. enter into an "open skies" agreement to inspect each other's military installations from the air, but Russia rejected the idea.

Despite a heart attack in 1955 and an abdominal operation in 1956, Eisenhower ran for reelection in 1956. Campaigning with his familiar genial smile and arms upraised, he heard the chant of "We Like Ike" from coast to coast. He won with a greater landslide than in 1952, receiving 457 electoral votes to 73 for Stevenson.

Eisenhower's second term was marked by more difficulties than the first. In 1957 he sent troops to force integration of schools in Little Rock, Arkansas. The successful Russian Sputnik, launched in October 1957, was a blow to U.S. prestige, but the American Explorer I satellite was launched soon afterward in January 1958. Eisenhower broke off relations with Cuba when Premier Fidel Castro seized American property on the island.

After leaving office Eisenhower retired to his Gettysburg farm. On March 28, 1969, he died of heart failure.

John Fitzgerald Kennedy

Jan. 20,
1961
-
Nov. 22,
1963

Charming, youthful, handsome John F. Kennedy entered the White House at the age of forty-three, the youngest man to win a presidential election. He was also the first Roman Catholic to occupy the White House. His attractive wife Jacqueline was thirty-one when she became First Lady.

That such a promising career should end in dismal tragedy seemed impossible for a stunned nation to comprehend when President Kennedy was shot to death on a street in Dallas, Texas.

John F. Kennedy was born in Brookline, Mass., May 29, 1917. He was the second of eight children, the son of millionaire Joseph P. Kennedy who had served as ambassador to Great Britain under Franklin Roosevelt. The elder Kennedy had resigned this post in protest against the foreign policies of President Roosevelt.

John attended the Canterbury School in New Milford, Conn., then went to Choate Academy in Wallingford, Conn. When he graduated from Choate in 1935, he was voted "most likely to succeed." He attended Princeton University briefly, then majored

in government and international relations at Harvard. After a summer tour of Europe in 1939, Kennedy wrote his college thesis on the failure of England to prepare itself against Nazi Germany. Published in book form in 1940, under the title, *Why England Slept,* the work became a best seller. Kennedy graduated *cum laude* from Harvard this same year.

Before Pearl Harbor, Kennedy enlisted as a seaman in the Navy. In 1942 he was assigned to a PT boat squadron. He was commissioned an ensign and commanded a boat which patrolled the Solomon Islands. A Japanese destroyer cut his boat in half, and Kennedy's heroic rescue of survivors of his crew won him the Navy and Marine Corps Medal as well as the Purple Heart.

After the war, Kennedy worked as a reporter for the Hearst newspapers for a short time. One of his assignments was coverage of the United Nations conference at San Francisco in 1945. He decided to enter politics in 1946, and with the enthusiastic help of his brothers and sisters won the Democratic nomination to the House of Representatives in the eleventh district of Massachusetts. His mother and sisters organized teas at the homes of voters, while his father furnished campaign funds. He won the election and as a Congressman voted for Truman's welfare programs, including expanded social security benefits, aid to veterans, and old-age benefits. He opposed the Taft-Hartley Act, feeling it was anti-labor.

In 1952, Kennedy upset the veteran Re-

1960

ELECTORAL VOTE
TOTAL 537

MINOR .7%

POPULAR VOTE
TOTAL 68,836,385

DEMOCRATIC (KENNEDY)

REPUBLICAN (NIXON)

INDEPENDENT (BYRD)

publican Senator Henry Cabot Lodge by winning his seat in the U.S. Senate.

Kennedy married Jacqueline Lee Bouvier, daughter of a wealthy Wall Street broker, in 1953. Meanwhile, as a Massachusetts Senator, he worked for bills that would help New England industries. During this time his book about U.S. statesmen, *Profiles in Courage,* published in 1956, became a best seller and won the Pulitzer prize for biography in 1957.

He and his family began working tirelessly for his presidential nomination as early as 1956. At the 1960 Democrat convention in Los Angeles, he won the nomination on the first ballot. In the ensuing campaign, he and Vice-President Richard Nixon appeared on four nation-wide TV debates. Kennedy won by a slim 112,000 out of some 68 million votes cast. It was one of the closest elections in U.S. history.

As president Kennedy fought for Negro rights. He established the Peace Corps which sends Americans to assist the people in underdeveloped countries with education, modern farming and industrial methods. On April 17, 1961, an attempt of exiled Cubans to invade the island and overthrow Castro resulted in disaster. Kennedy admitted responsibility for this failure. Later that year he met with Russian Premier Khrushchev in Vienna in an effort to settle differences, but the meeting was fruitless.

A buildup of Russian missile bases in Cuba prompted Kennedy to challenge the Soviet Union in 1962. He ordered a naval blockade of the island, and told Russia the missile sites must be dismantled. Though Russia apparently backed down, the U.S. failed to make any on-site inspection, and many experts believed that some missiles still remained in Cuba.

On a speaking tour which took him to Dallas, Texas, Kennedy was shot as he rode in a motorcade. The accused assassin was Lee Harvey Oswald, a psychologically unstable pro-Castro Marxist. Kennedy fell into the arms of his wife, who was riding in the open car beside him.

The shocked nation and the world sorrowfully recalled the ringing words of Kennedy's inaugural address: "Ask not what your country can do for you — ask what you can do for your country."

Lyndon Baines Johnson

After making a career in Congress for more than twenty years, Lyndon Johnson accepted the vice-presidential nomination in 1960 partly as a way to enjoy a less strenuous schedule. Then in a split second, on November 22, 1963, he was forced to take over the most strenuous and arduous job in the world.

Johnson was born in Stonewall, Texas, August 27, 1908. He was the son of Sam Johnson and Rebekah Baines Johnson. His father's family had been associated with Texas politics for many years. In high school, Lyndon was an enthusiastic member of the debating team, and although he was never an outstanding scholar, he was always in the thick of classroom discussions.

After a brief period of seeking odd jobs in California, he entered Southwest Texas State College in San Marcos, and graduated in 1930. For a time he taught public speaking and debating at the Sam Houston High School in Houston, Texas. Then in 1931 he had his first taste of politics when he worked for the Congressional election of Richard M. Kleberg. Kleberg won and took Johnson to Washington as his secretary.

In the meantime he became a close friend of Sam Rayburn, who was speaker of the House. With Rayburn's support, he was appointed administrator of the National Youth Administration in Texas. This was 1935, in the depth of the Great Depression. He ran for Congress, in 1938, backing Franklin Roosevelt and the New Deal and won by a wide margin. All during Franklin Roosevelt's administration, Lyndon Johnson had the president's ear and his influence.

After Johnson lost a bid for the U.S. Senate in a special election in 1941, the Japanese attacked Pearl Harbor, Johnson became the first member of the House of Representatives to serve in the armed forces. In 1942 he was sent as a lieutenant

commander in the Navy to inspect Pacific operations.

After World War II, in 1948, Johnson won a close election to the U.S. Senate. In the upper house, he worked for strong national defense measures.

Senator Lyndon Johnson became universally admired and liked in Washington. His energy, warmth, and his folksy approach to people won him a host of friends. He had a knack of persuading even his political opponents to his point of view.

After recovering from a heart attack in 1955, he took an active part in the 1956 presidential campaign for Adlai Stevenson. Then, in 1960, he worked hard to win the presidential nomination. When John F. Kennedy won the nomination and asked Johnson to be his running mate, he at first refused, then agreed.

On November 22, 1963, riding in the presidential motorcade through the heart of Dallas, Texas, he heard the reports of a gun. A moment later, a secret service man pushed him roughly to the floor of the car. With the tragic assassination of Kennedy,

Student and Peace
Demonstrations 1964-67

Negro Riots in
U.S. Cities 1964-67

War on Poverty
(OEC) Begun 1964

ATLANTIC CITY
Nominated
for President
1964

"Hawks vs. Doves"
Vietnam War Debate 1965-67

WASHINGTON
Representative 1937-1948
Senator 1949-1961

LOS ANGELES
Nominated for Vice President
1960

Civil Rights Bills Passed
1964, '65, '66

Medicare Program 1965

DALLAS
Sworn in as President After
Kennedy's Assassination 1963

STONEWALL
Birthplace 1908

Johnson City

HOUSTON
High School Teacher 1930-1932

U.S. Commits Combat
Troops to Vietnam Conflict
March 1965

SAN ANTONIO
Married Claudia "Lady Bird"
Taylor 1934

SAN MARCOS
Graduated from Southwest
Texas State Teachers College 1930

U.S. Troops Intervene
in Dominican Rep. Crisis 1965

Lyndon Johnson had suddenly become President of the United States. He was sworn in at Love Field, Dallas, in the presidential airplane, shortly after 2:00 P.M. that same day.

While the nation mourned, Johnson moved swiftly and efficiently to bring about smooth transition in the government. His early programs included cuts in government expenditures; a bill reducing income tax which had been supported by President Kennedy; and enactment of a civil rights law. In 1964 Johnson was elected President in his own right. He defeated Senator Barry Goldwater of Arizona by the largest popular vote in American history.

After his election, Johnson moved more decisively toward an administration of his own design. He worked ceaselessly for legislation to provide health insurance for the aged and federal funds for education. To popularize his program of welfare legislation, Johnson spoke eloquently of a future "great society" and declared "unconditional war on poverty in America."

Meanwhile, the other war in Vietnam grew to major proportions. In 1964 only a few thousand American military advisers were in Vietnam training South Vietnamese troops. By the latter part of 1965 there were 180,000 American combat troops in Vietnam. As the war escalated our commitment continued to grow until it totaled over 475,000 men in 1967. At the same time expenditures for this undeclared and controversial war bit deeply into the national budget. Many of Johnson's domestic plans — particularly those involving the war on poverty — were seriously curtailed. A dollar drain abroad and threats of more racial unrest and inflation at home were added shoals that faced the nation and its 36th president.

Then, on March 31, 1968, at the end of a nationwide television speech, in which he announced a reduction in the bombing of North Vietnam, Johnson also announced that he would not run for re-election.

1964

ELECTORAL VOTE
TOTAL 538

POPULAR VOTE
TOTAL 70,640,289

DEMOCRATIC (JOHNSON)

REPUBLICAN (GOLDWATER)

85

Richard Milhous Nixon

Jan. 20
1969

War II, Nixon left his law practice in Whittier to work briefly for the government in Washington. In August 1942, he received a commission in the Navy as a lieutenant, junior grade. After repeated requests for sea duty, he was finally attached to the South Pacific Combat Air Transport Command where he earned the rank of lieutenant commander. At the end of the war a friend asked him to run in the 12th Congressional District of California. To everyone's surprise, he won handily and was re-elected two years later.

In 1948-49, serving in the House Un-American Activities Committee, Nixon achieved national prominence by spearheading the investigation which led to the conviction of Alger Hiss for perjury on his testimony about communist affiliations. Nixon was elected to the United States Senate in 1950, and two years later was selected by Dwight Eisenhower as the general's vice-presidential running mate.

When he became Vice-President under Eisenhower, Nixon traveled abroad as a special emissary for the President. In 1955, Eisenhower suffered a heart attack and Nixon was suddenly thrown into a role with new responsibilities. In 1956, Eisenhower's recovery made possible his bid for re-election. He and Nixon again carried the Republicans to a landslide victory, and Nixon continued to serve as Vice-President in an expanded role. In 1959, he visited the Soviet Union and met with Khrushchev.

The Republican candidate who became the 37th President of the United States, Richard Milhous Nixon, staged what many analysts consider to be one of the most amazing comebacks in American political history. Defeated for the presidency in 1960 by John F. Kennedy, soundly defeated in a bid for the governorship of California in 1962 by Democrat Pat Brown, the former Vice-President Nixon had bitterly announced to a press conference that he would never again run for public office.

But Richard Nixon's destiny was inextricably bound to the world of politics, and it seemed that all his life had been a prelude to achieving the highest office in the land. Born January 9, 1913, in the California town of Yorba Linda, he was the second of five sons of Francis and Hannah Milhous Nixon. In 1934, he graduated second in his class from Whittier College, then went to law school on a scholarship at Duke University. He received his LL.D. in 1937.

Nixon married Patricia Ryan in 1940. When America became embroiled in World

"Farewell" to politics after losing race for Governor of California 1962

Nomination for Vice-President 1952 and for President 1960
CHICAGO

TV debates 1960 Presidential campaign

NEW YORK
Joined New York law firm 1963

WASHINGTON
Representative   1947-1950
Senator   1951-1952
Vice-President   1953-1961

graduated from Whittier College 1934
WHITTIER

Married Patricia Ryan 1940

Law degree Duke University 1937

YORBA LINDA
Birthplace 1913

MIAMI
Nomination for President 1968

The 1960 Republican convention chose Nixon to run against John F. Kennedy. After a campaign marked by a series of nationwide television debates, Kennedy won in an extremely close vote. Despite the disappointment of this setback, Nixon campaigned for the governorship of California in 1962 and was defeated.

At this point Nixon retired from the public scene to practice law in New York City. For several years the electorate heard little about him. But in spite of his self-imposed exile from politics, after the overwhelming defeat of Barry Goldwater by Lyndon Johnson in 1964, Nixon began quietly to help rebuild and reunite the badly shattered Republican party.

When the presidential primaries began in the spring of 1968, Nixon engaged in an active campaign to win delegates to the Republican National Convention. At the Miami Convention, Nixon received the nomination on the first ballot.

A three-way campaign developed among Nixon, his Democratic opponent, Vice-President Hubert H. Humphrey, and George C. Wallace, candidate for the American Independent Party. Despite the divided vote, Nixon won the election with 301 electoral votes.

Nixon's tenure in the White House, so far, has been marked by a de-escalation of the war in Vietnam, and the gradual return home of combat troops.

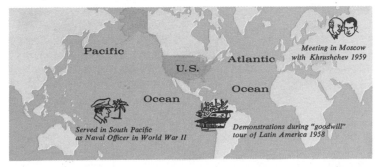

Meeting in Moscow with Khrushchev 1959

Served in South Pacific as Naval Officer in World War II

Demonstrations during "goodwill" tour of Latin America 1958

On the home front the Nixon administration had to deal with a wage-price inflationary spiral which did not yield even in the face of an economic recession. By early 1971, midpoint in President Nixon's term of office, the business picture showed signs of a comeback.

87

Laws Pertaining to the Presidency

THE CONSTITUTION

ARTICLE II The Presidency

SECTION. 1. The executive Power shall be vested in a President of the United States of America. He shall hold his Office during the Term of four Years, and, together with the Vice President, chosen for the same Term, be elected, as follows

Each State shall appoint, in such Manner as the Legislature thereof may direct, a Number of Electors, equal to the whole Number of Senators and Representatives to which the State may be entitled in the Congress: but no Senator or Representative, or Person holding an Office of Trust or Profit under the United States, shall be appointed an Elector.

The Electors shall meet in their respective States, and vote by Ballot for two Persons, of whom one at least shall not be an Inhabitant of the same State with themselves. And they shall make a List of all the Persons voted for, and of the Number of Votes for each; which List they shall sign and certify, and transmit sealed to the Seat of the Government of the United States, directed to the President of the Senate. The President of the Senate shall, in the Presence of the Senate and House of Representatives, open all the Certificates, and the votes shall then be counted. The Person having the greatest Number of Votes shall be the President, if such Number be a Majority of the whole Number of Electors appointed; and if there be more than one who have such Majority, and have an equal Number of Votes, then the House of Representatives shall immediately chuse by Ballot one of them for President; and if no person have a Majority, then from the five highest on the List the said House shall in like Manner chuse the President. But, in chusing the President, the Votes shall be taken by States, the Representation from each State having one Vote; A quorum for this purpose shall consist of a Member or Members from two thirds of the States, and a Majority of all the States shall be necessary to a Choice. In every Case, after the Choice of the President, the Person having the greatest Number of Votes of the Electors shall be the Vice President. But if there should remain two or more who have equal Votes, the Senate shall chuse from them by Ballot the Vice President.

The Congress may determine the Time of chusing the Electors, and the Day on which they shall give their Votes; which Day shall be the same throughout the United States.

No person except a natural born Citizen, or a Citizen of the United States, at the time of the Adoption of this Constitution, shall be eligible to the Office of President; neither shall any Person be eligible to that Office who shall not have attained to the Age of thirty five Years, and been fourteen Years a Resident within the United States.

In Case of the Removal of the President from Office, or of his Death, Resignation, or Inability to discharge the Powers and Duties of the said Office, the Same shall devolve on the Vice President, and the Congress may by Law provide for the Case of Removal, Death, Resignation or Inability, both of the President and Vice President, declaring what Officer shall then act as President, and such Officer shall act accordingly, until the Disability be removed, or a President shall be elected.

The President shall, at stated Times, receive for his Services, a Compensation, which shall neither be encreased nor diminished during the Period for which he shall have been elected, and he shall not receive within that Period any other Emolument from the United States, or any of them.

Before he enter on the Execution of his Office, he shall take the following Oath or Affirmation:— "I do solemnly swear (or affirm) that I will faithfully execute the Office of President of the United States, and will to the best of my Ability, preserve, protect and defend the Constitution of the United States."

SECTION. 2. The President shall be Commander in Chief of the Army and Navy of the United States, and of the Militia of the several States, when called into the actual Service of the United States; he may require the Opinion, in writing, of the principal Officer in each of the executive Departments, upon any Subject relating to the Duties of their respective Offices, and he shall have Power to grant Reprieves and Pardons for Offences against the United States, except in Cases of Impeachment.

He shall have Power, by and with the Advice and Consent of the Senate, to make Treaties, provided two thirds of the Senators present concur; and he shall nominate, and by and with the

Advice and Consent of the Senate, shall appoint Ambassadors, other public Ministers and Consuls, Judges of the supreme Court, and all other Officers of the United States, whose Appointments are not herein otherwise provided for, and which shall be established by Law: but the Congress may by Law vest the Appointment of such inferior Officers, as they think proper, in the President alone, in the Courts of Law, or in the Heads of Departments.

The President shall have Power to fill up all Vacancies that may happen during the Recess of the Senate, by granting Commissions which shall expire at the End of their next Session.

SECTION. 3. He shall from time to time give to the Congress Information of the State of the Union, and recommend to their Consideration such Measures as he shall judge necessary and expedient; he may, on extraordinary Occasions, convene both Houses, or either of them, and in Case of Disagreement between them, with Respect to the Time of Adjournment, he may adjourn them to such Time as he shall think proper; he shall receive Ambassadors and other public Ministers; he shall take Care that the Laws be faithfully executed, and shall Commission all the Officers of the United States.

SECTION. 4. The President, Vice-President and all civil Officers of the United States, shall be removed from Office on Impeachment for, and Conviction of, Treason, Bribery, or other high Crimes and Misdemeanors.

rected to the President of the Senate:—The President of the Senate shall, in the presence of the Senate and House of Representatives, open all the certificates and the votes shall then be counted; —The person having the greatest number of votes for President, shall be the President, if such number be a majority of the whole number of Electors appointed; and if no person have such majority, then from the persons having the highest numbers not exceeding three on the list of those voted for as President, the House of Representatives shall choose immediately, by ballot, the President. But in choosing the President, the votes shall be taken by states, the representation from each state having one vote; a quorum for this purpose shall consist of a member or members from two-thirds of the states, and a majority of all the states shall be necessary to a choice. And if the House of Representatives shall not choose a President whenever the right of choice shall devolve upon them, before the fourth day of March next following, then the Vice-President shall act as President, as in the case of the death or other constitutional disability of the President. — The person having the greatest number of votes as Vice-President, shall be the Vice-President, if such number be a majority of the whole number of Electors appointed, and if no person have a majority, then from the two highest numbers on the list, the Senate shall choose the Vice-President, a quorum for the purpose shall consist of two-thirds of the whole number of Senators, and a majority of the whole number shall be necessary to a choice. But no person constitutionally ineligible to the office of President shall be eligible to that of Vice-President of the United States.

AMENDMENTS TO THE CONSTITUTION

AMENDMENT 12. Presidential Elections (1804)

The Electors shall meet in their respective states, and vote by ballot for President and Vice-President, one of whom, at least, shall not be an inhabitant of the same state with themselves; they shall name in their ballots the person voted for as President, and in distinct ballots the person voted for as Vice-President, and they shall make distinct lists of all persons voted for as President, and of all persons voted for as Vice-President, and of the number of votes for each, which lists they shall sign and certify, and transmit sealed to the seat of the government of the United States, di-

AMENDMENT 20. Terms of Office (1933)

SECTION 1. The terms of the President and Vice President shall end at noon on the twentieth day of January, and the terms of Senators and Representatives at noon on the 3d day of January, of the years in which such terms would have ended if this article had not been ratified; and the terms of their successors shall then begin.

SECTION 2. The Congress shall assemble at least once in every year, and such meeting shall begin at noon on the 3d day of January, unless they shall by law appoint a different day.

SECTION 3. If, at the time fixed for the beginning of the term of the President, the President elect shall have died, the Vice President elect shall become President. If a President shall not have been chosen before the time fixed for the beginning of his term, or if the President elect shall have failed to qualify, then the Vice President elect shall act as President until a President shall have qualified; and the Congress may by law provide for the case wherein neither a President elect nor a Vice President elect shall have qualified, declaring who shall then act as President, or the manner in which one who is to act shall be selected, and such person shall act accordingly until a President or Vice President shall have qualified.

SECTION 4. The Congress may by law provide for the case of the death of any of the persons from whom the House of Representatives may choose a President whenever the right of choice shall have devolved upon them, and for the case of the death of any of the persons from whom the Senate may choose a Vice President whenever the right of choice shall have devolved upon them.

SECTION 5. Sections 1 and 2 shall take effect on the 15th day of October following the ratification of this article.

SECTION 6. This article shall be inoperative unless it shall have been ratified as an amendment to the Constitution by the legislatures of three-fourths of the several States within seven years from the date of its submission.

AMENDMENT 22. Number of Terms for a President (1951)

SECTION 1. No person shall be elected to the office of the President more than twice, and no person who has held the office of President, or acted as President, for more than two years of a term to which some other person was elected President shall be elected to the office of the President more than once. But this Article shall not apply to any person holding the office of President when this Article was proposed by the Congress, and shall not prevent any person who may be holding the office of President, or acting as President, during the term within which this Article becomes operative from holding the office of President or acting as President during the remainder of such term.

SECTION 2. This Article shall be inoperative unless it shall have been ratified as an amendment to the Constitution by the legislatures of three-fourths of the several states within seven years from the date of its submission to the States by the Congress.

AMENDMENT 23. Presidential Voting in the District of Columbia (1961)

SECTION 1. The District constituting the seat of Government of the United States shall appoint in such manner as the Congress may direct:

A number of electors of President and Vice President equal to the whole number of Senators and Representatives in Congress to which the District would be entitled if it were a State, but in no event more than the least populous State; they shall be in addition to those appointed by the States, but they shall be considered, for the purposes of the election of President and Vice President, to be electors appointed by a State; and they shall meet in the District and perform such duties as provided by the twelfth article of amendment.

SECTION 2. The Congress shall have power to enforce this article by appropriate legislation.

AMENDMENT 24. Barring Poll Tax in Federal Elections (1964)

SECTION 1. The right of citizens of the United States to vote in any primary or other election for President or Vice President, for electors for President or Vice President, or for Senator or Representative in Congress, shall not be denied or abridged by the United States or any State by reason of failure to pay any poll tax or other tax.

SECTION 2. The Congress shall have the power to enforce this article by appropriate legislation.

AMENDMENT 25. Presidential Disability and Succession (1967)

SECTION 1. In the case of the removal of the President from office or his death or resignation, the Vice President shall become President.

SECTION 2. Whenever there is a vacancy in the office of the Vice President, the President shall nominate a Vice President who shall take the office upon confirmation by a majority vote of both houses of Congress.

SECTION 3. Whenever the President transmits to the President pro tempore of the Senate and the Speaker of the House of Representatives his written declaration that he is unable to discharge the powers and duties of his office, and until he transmits to them a written declaration to the contrary, such powers and duties shall be discharged by the Vice President as Acting President.

SECTION 4. Whenever the Vice President and a majority of either the principal officers of the executive departments or of such other body as Congress may by law provide, transmit to the President pro tempore of the Senate and the Speaker of the House of Representatives their written declaration that the President is unable to discharge the powers and duties of his office, the Vice President shall immediately assume the powers and duties of the office as Acting President.

Thereafter, when the President transmits to the President pro tempore of the Senate and the Speaker of the House of Representatives his written declaration that no inability exists, he shall resume the powers and duties of his office unless the Vice President and a majority of either the principal officers of the executive department or of such other body as Congress may by law provide, transmit within four days to the President pro tempore of the Senate and the Speaker of the House of Representatives their written declaration that the President is unable to discharge the powers and duties of his office. Thereupon Congress shall decide the issue, assembling within forty-eight hours for that purpose if not in session. If the Congress, within twenty-one days after receipt of the latter written declaration, or, if Congress is not in session, within twenty-one days after Congress is required to assemble, determines by two-thirds vote of both houses that the President is unable to discharge the powers and duties of his office the Vice President shall continue to discharge the same as Acting President; otherwise, the President shall resume the powers and duties of his office.

LAW OF PRESIDENTIAL SUCCESSION

UNITED STATES CODE, Title 3, Chapter 1
(pertinent portions)

§ 19 Vacancy in offices of both President and
Vice President; officers eligible to act

(a) (1) If, by reason of death, resignation, removal from office, inability, or failure to qualify, there is neither a President nor Vice President to discharge the powers and duties of the office of President, then the Speaker of the House of Representatives shall, upon his resignation as Speaker and as Representative in Congress, act as President.

(2) The same rule shall apply in the case of death, resignation, removal from office, or inability of an individual acting as President under this subsection.

(b) If, at the time when under subsection (a) of this section a Speaker is to begin the discharge of the powers and duties of the office of President, there is no Speaker, or the Speaker fails to qualify as Acting President, then the President pro tempore of the Senate shall, upon his resignation as President pro tempore and as Senator, act as President.

(c) An individual acting as President under subsection (a) or subsection (b) of this section shall continue to act until the expiration of the then current Presidential term, except that (1) if his discharge of the powers and duties of the office is founded in whole or in part on the failure of both the President-elect and the Vice President-elect to qualify, then he shall act only until a President or Vice President qualifies; and (2) if his discharge of the powers and duties of the office is founded in whole or in part on the inability of the President or Vice President, then he shall act only until the removal of the disability of one of such individuals.

(d) (1) If, by reason of death, resignation, removal from office, inability, or failure to qualify, there is no President pro tempore to act as President under subsection (b) of this section, then the officer of the United States who is highest on the following list, and who is not under disability to discharge the powers and duties of the office of President shall act as President: Secretary of State, Secretary of the Treasury, Secretary of Defense, Attorney General, Postmaster General, Secretary of the Interior, Secretary of Agriculture, Secretary of Commerce, Secretary of Labor. (June 25, 1948, ch. 644, 62 Stat. 677.)

§ 20 Resignation or refusal of office

The only evidence of a refusal to accept, or of a resignation of the office of President or Vice President, shall be an instrument in writing, declaring the same, and subscribed by the person refusing to accept or resigning, as the case may be, and delivered into the office of the Secretary of State. (June 25, 1948, ch. 644, 62 Stat. 678.)

Index

THE PRESIDENT'S FLAG

THE WHITE HOUSE